MW01226108

Bangkok Baby

The Inside Story

Of

Ladyboys

Sky TV's acclaimed series

David Bonnie

Copyright

Bangkok Baby - The Inside Story of Ladyboys

Sky TV's acclaimed documentary series

1st edition 2014

Text by David Bonnie

ISBN 978-1-63323-196-2

eISBN 978-1-63323-195-5

Published by BooksMango

E-mail: info@booksmango.com

Text & cover page Copyright© David Bonnie

No part of this book may be reproduced, copied, stored or transmitted in any form without prior written permission from the publisher.

***

Contents

Book One

Bangkok Baby

Loving the Loveless Ladyboys Of Bangkok
Bangkok, night and day, light and dark. A city that cannot be
defined, just like the beautiful ladyboys who work and live there.
A journey through the dark into the light and back again. Follow
the author on a nine-month ride through the city and down the deep
soi of imagination, lust, love and sexuality. It may be the ride you
expect.

Prelude

The sound of a farang (white foreigner) shouting at a bar girl who has poured too much coke in his drink makes you look to your left and the Big Dog bar. The girl speaks no English so perhaps this is among her first weeks in Bangkok. Music is playing very loudly in the bar, 'I met a gin soaked barroom queen in Memphis, she tried to take me upstairs for a ride'. The girl looks frightened.

The smoke of the barbecue's mixes with the stink of the rotting garbage, stale sweat and piss.

Decay, degradation and the faces of the Thai vendors and motorcycle taxi drivers are etched into the grey concrete at the entrance to Soi 4 like an ancient economic truth.

Their look is not envious, nor jealous and not full of hate; but the look of those trapped in the waking dream world of constant and chronic poverty. They are the faces of the drowned and drowning.

'It's the ho, o, o, nky tonk women, give me, give, give me the honky tonk blues'.

This is Bangkok. This is Nana.

But you are looking past the messy third-world order of cracked and dirty tarmac and paving slabs that border the car park. You have lived long enough to know that under the surface of things lays the dream reality that you seek.

Bangkok; full of men and women with plans to escape back to Surin, Korat, Leeds or Texas; just as soon as they have enough money or less desire. But what you see is something tender in the way Bangkok holds its residents. In the impossibly beautiful bodies and faces of the Ladyboys arriving as dusk sets in, in their eyes, in the way they hold themselves. In their gaze, you see a story.

And then, just as night arrives you see them at the entrance to the plaza. A man is on his knees at the feet of a Ladyboy. She is 6 feet tall and her face has the kind of dark beauty that can destroy worlds.

You cannot hear his words but the sounds he makes are more animal than human. Even on his knees the man still has a stiff pride, the quality of an iron weathervane, always pointing towards her, his North. His supplication, his willingness to beg comes from strength not weakness. He does not see the people that flow around him.

The Ladyboy holds her arms across her chest as she looks down at him. Her face is set like a beautiful oriental mask; without expression. She turns on a heel and walks away. He screams after her, 'Faridaaa'. She does not slow her stride as she walks towards you but as the rain explodes onto the street you see a single tear run down her face. Then she is gone. This is the foretelling of a future that has been waiting to happen for so long.

I cannot say what happens to the man you saw or the Ladyboy. I can only tell you how it began.

This is a love story of Bangkok.

One-Bangkok, Day One.

I knew something big was going to happen today.

I came up from a deep sleep to alert, gasping for breath. I was dreaming about falling and just before I hit the ground I woke up . . . and started laughing to myself . . . I couldn't stop laughing. I was lying in a room of the Royal Asia Hotel, Sukhumvit soi 8, Bangkok.

Yesterday, was it yesterday? I was in England. How could I be so far away from what I knew in such a short space of time? My laughter began to sound like panic . . .even to me. I was completely alone . . . having left everything and everyone I know behind!

I suddenly heard my father's voice . . . 'You need backbone to live the life you want', Stop thinking!

He was Sergeant Major of the 11th Hussars before he died last year. I miss him.

The day passed without a ripple but under the surface I was ticking and tight, waiting for the night to come. I knew I was going to take a giant step, a step that would set me free.

I had seen Ladyboys online and these creatures fascinated me. I tried to understand why?

I am way past 21 and have never entertained the idea of gay sex. No. not even a little. I remember when I was a soldier hearing a story about some guys from my Company who got tricked by some Ladyboys in the Philippines. As the denouement of the story was spun in which the boys in question reviled and spurned the evil Ladyboys, who had been described as indescribably beautiful . . .I said . . . I would have fucked them anyway!

I was a lot more naive back then.

At 14 I had the album cover of Bowie's Aladdin Sane on my wall and remember having a vague but curious fascination with his feminine

looks. 'They laughed at his long black hair, his feminine grace . . .
.wow, what a throw forward to Thai Ladyboys!

By the time I arrived in Bangkok I had been running for years. Running towards and away from things and through things. Away from stifling expectation and any kind of 'ordinariness', towards adventure, through life, love and through the lives of so many women I cannot count them. Always moving on, never settling for 'comfortable' searching for something I do not understand. I only ever stayed rooted long enough to bring up my sons.

I knew this night was coming. I could rationalise my fascination with ladyboys by saying things like, I have been married three times and look how that turned out, maybe I will be luckier with a ladyboy? That would be disingenuous and I can no longer be that man. I have had some great relationships with women; one true love and broken hearts and had mine broken too. I cannot complain about women I just never found and kept a real partnership of mind and body.

So I headed out to Nana Plaza for the first time ever.

Walking from Soi 8 the night seemed to open itself before me and swallow me into this new world. I was alive. I did not stop at the bars inside Nana or with the girls I met along the way, it felt as if my body knew the way so I stopped thinking and planning. I walked up the stairs in the corner of Nana Entertainment Plaza and at the top someone was waiting for me. She was tall, dark, beautiful and looking me in the eyes. I am 6ft 5inch. She said hello, asked me if I want to come inside with her. I followed without question. I was transfixed. We entered Casanova's and colour and sound exploded on me like a giant bomb made of everything desirable and gorgeous there is in the world. I was the only Man (note the capital) in the place. My leader led me by the hand to a table and leather lounger . . . and I began to get some focus back enough to see the dancers were the most exciting animals I had ever seen.

I was so mesmerised that at first I did not notice that the girl who
bought me in was asking for a drink and but I did notice her she was
speaking to me from the bottom of a swimming pool, refracted, out
of focus. I was too far gone to care . . . I did not want her . . .I wanted
the girl looking in my eyes as she thrust her groin at me and smiling
as she did it.

Nadia the beautiful!

I smiled at her. I was green but not intimidated by the Amazons who watched and waited, kneaded and cooed.

But strange and exciting things have always happened to me, I am lucky that way and now everything seemed to begin to speed up and the girl who bought me in jumped up and cursed at me, 'Fucker', which made me laugh and smile even more. She tore off her dress and jumped onto the podium where she started a vengeful dance routine . . . designed to make me regret the moment I chose someone else.

Another even more goddess like Ladyboy walked over to me and struck an awe inspiring (but tongue in cheek) pose inches from my face and then, mimicking her angry friend also tore off her dress. What a body!!!!! She looked me in the eyes with a challenge . . .but, but, but I called out for Nadia and after pointing at herself in a mock 'really, you want me?' performance she jumped off the podium and into my life. Well, for an hour of it at least!

300bht for the short-time room upstairs plus 600bht Bar Fine and 1500bht to her are the financial details.

We began with lots of kissing and I don't mean dry kissing, I was so excited by this girl. The sex began with her giving me a blowjob, no condom and lots of touching. She has great tits and smooth, smooth skin.

Hers was about to be the first cock I had ever sucked. I told her so. She was only slightly impressed; expect she's heard that one before? I did not make her come but liked the sucking . . . it did not seem to matter if it is a cock or a pussy. The idea is, I guess, to give pleasure to someone whom you really fancy so it doesn't really matter how one goes about that?

Nadia put the condom on Johnny Farang with her mouth like a good girl and we commenced to fuck. Finding her LB Pussy was no problem as it was her asshole, and I know where to look for them. After some medium strength penetration I decided I needed more purchase and so my princess assumed the crouching lioness position. Things got violent and hazy at this point as all the blood rushed to my cock but I fucked her like I had been doing it all my life (except I also had her cock in my hand, well until I lost control!)

I arrived in a whooping, moaning kind of a way followed by a kind of hysterical laughter that sometimes happens while my brain unscrambles itself and I pull back from the edge of something that feels a little like death? This is a sign that I have had a very, very good time.

I have tried explaining the laughter to frightened females in the past with only comparative success. Nadia was not fazed; she is made of sterner stuff. What a woman!

She showered me and as we dressed I tried to talk to her without too much of a stupid, happy smile on my face because I loved her now, and we left together. As we passed the 'receptionists' of the hotel she gave them 100 baht and she turned around to me as she walked down the stairs and looking up, wrinkled her nose in the cutest way and said, 'Because I have a soft heart'. I said, 'Yes, you do have a soft heart, but you have a hard cock Nadia and for that, thanks are due!

That's how I lost my Ladyboy virginity and discovered that I still had a heart.

Two-Bangkok, Week One.

I met a 'good girl' twice. She works for a diamond dealer in Silom. She is such a cute Thai girl with beautiful Asian eyes, Aommy has a delicate beauty and seems to be begging for her vineyards to be laid to waste by the devil in me. She has the kind of innocence that yearns to be desecrated. She brings out that terrible desire to actually 'fuck her to death'. The wish that one could come so hard that one could 'blow the back out of her'! The line we walk between sex and violence serves to remind us just what dangerous creatures we are.

We met at Siam Square where the fountain ejaculates into the air and adolescent Thai girls run between the jets dreaming of the day when a real cock will come all over them.

We eat in Paragon. Wow, can she eat for a little girl! The bill was 1000 baht but as I was cunt-struck I suavely paid the bill. (Not really sure what that means) As we parted I kissed her for the first time and there was definitely promise in her eyes. Unfortunately the promise soon became a goodbye wave from the other side of the Sky-Train platform. I boarded with a wet patch in my pants. Not piss, the other kind of stain. About this time I was communicating with a Ladyboy from Pattaya called Mona. You may know her? It was via Thai Love Links, an excellent site for action as long as you learn the rules of the game rapidly; preferably before you are standing at the bus station in Surin city with a suitcase full of presents for your new mum and dad, sisters, brothers, nieces, nephews.

Said Mona was becoming increasingly agitated concerning my promise to come to visit her in Pattaya, in fact she was becoming a little frightening. Not

that I am scared of a girl (I add hastily) but when I compared damage done to me by girls and that done to me by my brothers . . . the girls come out as undisputed champs!

I had a dream about a knife attack that night. I am sorry to say I was not the knife wielder in the attack but sadly, the recipient of Mona's vengeance. I began to think that this may be my fate should I disappoint her. Only a matter of time you say, and I agree, hanging my head in shame as I do. I am only a man with a cock.

I wandered down a friendly Soi looking for a friendly fuck and bumped into a girl with the most gorgeous face . . . .I asked her the directions to the nearest toilet and she took me there even obligingly holding the door open while I pissed. She was a curious girl and probably a little hungry too as customers were and are thin on the ground. She was not letting me out of her sights!

I agree to a massage in the fleapit she confessed to working at and in we went.

I love the oil, man; I cannot get enough of that stuff! And after some slippery slap and tickle, well rubbing and sliding actually it became condom time. Why do people always seem surprised when I say something like,' I want to fuck you now.' Am I missing some point of etiquette? Pen, for that was her name, appeared surprised enough to repeat my statement, 'You want to fuck me'? What a beautiful sentence that is!

She agreed but 'Oh dear' the condom is too small and after two rips and a couple of near strangulations of my best friend, we gave up. I have to admit to a degree of boastful pride, especially as she kept saying,' Too big, too big'. I was willing her to say, Too beaucoup, like in the film, you know, 'Saving Private Ryan', the scene when Tom Hanks tells the other soldiers about fucking his wife over the kitchen table. Alas she did not play along, I am in Vietnam now though so there is hope left! I realise now of course that the Thai condoms are made to fit Thai men; poor little buggers.

So offers of a different kind were made by the plucky girl faced with the task of bringing off such an enormous cock (ha ha) but I have always thought of hand/blow jobs as a kind of substitute sex that is acceptable only when the real thing is not available. Like wartime rationing when one had to accept sausages instead of real meat. Perhaps blow/hand jobs are the sausages of sex? No? I agree. That idea is going nowhere. I suppose I really think of those activities as an hors d'ouvre, to the entrée. Ok for a starter but not as a replacement. How many prawn cocktails can you eat? Or Asparagus in Dijon sauce if you are middle class.

I agreed to a blow/hand job because as I looked at her pretty face I felt the urge to come all over it. I knelt on the mattress on the floor of the booth we were soiling and she stroked me off with an oily fist . . . the booths were only separated by a curtain (fucking hell) and someone else was humping away on the other side of mine. Anyway after a few minutes I unloaded all over Pen's oily tits with a hollow shout that made the humper next door freeze like a meerkhat on his mound. Silence. Then he resumed his monotonous activity with what seemed the enthusiasm of a miner returning to the coalface after a tea break.

On my way home I met the girls of the street bar next to the Asoke Sky-Train entrance. My eye was caught by Tan, as I later came to know her. She is the sexy minx of a mama-san but on that fateful night she was serving drinks the

whole time so I sat with Katy and got drunk before going to bed about 4am. I vowed to return and meet that mama-san later!

Three-Guess

I saw a video on YouTube that starred Jay the owner of Guess Bar at the time talking to another Ladyboy and ending the 'interview' by saying, 'You want to be my farang'? As I sat at my computer back in England I surprised myself by mumbling 'Yes, I do' under my breath. What was it about this girl and Ladyboys as a third sex that attracted me? Maybe the moments when they forget themselves when you make them laugh and their voice goes from falsetto to bass for a moment and how they cover it up. It's so endearing and exposes their vulnerability and bravery, it's impossible not to empathise.

But back there in England, I knew nothing of that; my body was the only thing responding to what it considered a very sexy animal.

Bangkok-Day 6: Guess Bar, the Holy Grail of my Ladyboy Quest. No Jay. She split with her farang boyfriend and moved back up-country. Exe was the new manager; a kind of sexy version of Pamela Anderson. Disappointment turned to fascination as I entered my heart's desire.

I was the only customer in there. Wow! A host of angels jostled for my attention standing around the too comfy leather sofa I sat in and pushing each other aside and pushing their groins into my face. All the names were there. You know them all. Gate sauntered by as only she can saunter, like a sexy but drunken sloth.

The best jostler was Aui, probably because it transpired that she does not take hormones so has her competitive male streak still intact! If you have seen her flit across the floor of Guess bar, lifting her skirt like Marilyn you will find it hard to believe but Aui is physically all male! As they all stood in front of me, I hooked my leg around Aui and she jumped down beside me as the other darlings looked for fresh blood. Aui's face is so pretty and feminine that I did not take long to go upstairs to the rooms above the bar. As we stripped for action she says to me, 'I same, same you, it ok?" in a really sexy voice that made me turn to see her reveal 'no tits at all'! Inside I was stunned, but I remembered my credo before my surprise even flashed across my face. 'Never say No!' I did not want to her to feel bad, I was already in love! (Of sorts) So now we fell onto the bed, a boy and his horse. No, wait, I didn't mean to say that! Yes, it's true she did remind me of a pony, with her pony -tail and high heels, but I don't have any desire to fuck horses you understand.

I am not responsible for my imagination. That's my next tattoo! Across the chest I think in big letters, just so everyone knows. She has got a healthy cock, that girl! Not quite as big as a farang cock but getting there and she was very frisky! Sucking and moaning ensued and she was hard and insistent. Remember, I had a go at sucking cock with Nadia from Casanova but as I was giving head to Aui I realised she was about to come. Fucking hell! What do I do now? I felt girlish (if you ever meet me this will make you laugh) OHHH! A mouthful of something naturally makes you swallow . . .doesn't it? I did. I swallowed come for the first time in my life. Wow, I felt really proud even when I needed a drink of water to wash it down. Aui smiled lazily as I drunk her water. That'll teach ya, I said! And now it's my turn!

Unfortunately I could not fuck her as she said, too big! That sentence is becoming a little too familiar and I am beginning to think it might not be true! Saying that, later in this series of reflections I will tell you about drawing ass blood from a certain LB so it could be true? Anyway, she told me she couldn't take hormones because they make her sick and she does not like the idea of surgery to give her some tits. She said she could not take it up the ass. I tried but it just would not fit! I had to accept that Aui's mouth was the only hole I was getting that night. I am not complaining, not at all. There is something so feminine and appealing about that girl . . . . .

Later Aui took to calling me at night asking if she could come over or would I meet her at a disco? Or, uttering sentences like, 'Me want go shopping wid you Emporium'. She's so naively mercenary it is endearing! She came over to the Tai-pan a few nights later and the same performance was repeated. I read that 60% of gay men experience pain during anal sex and report it as being the biggest sexual problem they ever experience. Understandable really. Aui suggested on one occasion that she fuck me and she could have too! Not for me thanks, but if any of you guys love that then she is most definitely your girl. So thanks Aui, for teaching me a valuable lesson.

Four

We met and her face collided with the back of my retina and left a permanent scar. It will last forever. Like being blinded by an eclipse. The rest of the world is forever in the shade.

Dark shadows of red and black shaped her face, an expensive piece of modern art that no one understands. Standing up close to her was like a private viewing in a gallery after lights out. Privilege in desolate isolation.

She was impervious to the surroundings like a queen slumming it for the night. When she spoke someone turned down the background volume. Her touch on my arm sent electric impulses singing across the synapses.

A few days later she asked me to come back to her room with her. I agreed, impressed, touched, falling.

We got off the Sky-Train at the fantastically named Wongwain Yai. She sat next to me on a 'little bus'. People stared. Her smooth, naked leg touched mine. I thought about animals.

There in her room she smiled for the first time. I told her she was pretty when she smiled. She's watched too many of Fashion TV's unsmiling, emaciated, spaced out, lost, fucked-up models. She needed a fix of joy and a week off from mirror-watch. Now she smiles more. Carries her mirror a little less. She is pretty when she smiles but I can still see the Thai dancer over her shoulder when she is holding her fingers just so and I can hear the melancholy, sing- song Yaksha wail in the air conditioners lull.

Every day when we were apart she asked if I 'had a dinner yet'. Eating is important to the Thai people. She eats like a pony-tailed horse. Now she pulls me by the hand at crossroads traffic snarl, keeps me out of trouble as if I had never walked on a street before. Calling me she puts a W where a V should be and still bears no reflection . . . on her life, her story, her gender as if she sprang from a shell in the Siam Sea, a transgender Venus.

I am going to stay a while in 2011, The Year of the Tiger.

Five

Forgive me as I jump forward in time to the present. Monday, December 27th 2010; the closing days of the year. I write on a bus to Surin City. Sitting beside me is the Ladyboy who grabbed my arm as I passed her back in October. I was a customer then but now, so much more and so much more complicated than our first meetings. I did not follow the three-day rule and now it is too late. I love her, without any doubt. That night, I came back from Phuket, sick with some kind of fever and sick at heart. Phuket made me think again about my love affair with Thailand. I met an American on the Sky-Train and helped him find his hotel. We planned to meet later and do the tour of Cowboy and Nana; his first time, my happy re- acquaintance. Once in Angel Witch he could not be moved and so I left him and began to walk home alone. As I left Nana, there she was, wearing the dress from Hell; that face and that voice that seemed familiar, challenging and tender all at the same time. "I want go with you', she demanded, as they all do. But as I refused she seemed to see that I was sick, or maybe she saw that I was very drunk. She gave me little choice and held my arm as she guided me to a street restaurant on the corner of soi 3/1. I needed to eat something to soak up the booze and the bitterness of Phuket that I had tried to drink out of my system. I staggered and she kept me out of the traffic. A scene that is played out all over Bangkok, Pattaya and Phuket so often that to observers it must look like Groundhog Day. We ate, talked. I sobered up a little. She took me home to the Tai-Pan and stayed. We slept until three. She fetched medicine. I called it the Green Tiger medicine even though it's white and now I know it's called, Katay Bin (Flying Rabbit.) She told me it cures all ills, especially of the stomach. Perhaps it was a love potion because although I cannot remember exactly when, somewhere between the second and third day my heart entered the proceedings. I was surprised. I thought I had said goodbye to all that horror years before but as she sleeps beside me on the bus I know that I have no choice but to play this deadly game out to the end or until the spell breaks.

Love has me wrapped up and takes all of my senses. Watching her straighten her hair is like looking at a Botticelli, a trip to the night market with her, a journey with Virgil. So much love I cannot hold it in, but so much having to accept what she does for a living. I can never afford to take care of her enough so that she can stop working. That is the knife, the razor blade to my throat. That is the living end that I have to make a beginning if we are to survive.

Now she is awake and so I have to look into her eyes again mesmerised.

Six-Surin City

The climate here in Surin is gentle, a breeze blows across the clean streets and shops. Even though it is landlocked, Surin has a seaside quality. Farida often talks of her mother so I am surprised that they do not embrace when they meet.

I ask her why and she says that she is shy. I tell her to make the most of the opportunity to do so; my mother died when I was her age.

Her father has the bright-eyed look and the emaciated body of an addict. Pictures of sisters and brothers, nephews and nieces rest on the cluttered shelves but there are none of her. Not one. I begin to understand all those character traits that surprised and sometimes saddened me. This girl is utterly alone, a survivor and now provider for the family that ignored her until she began to send money home every month. She told me that when she worked in a department store she did not earn enough to support her mum.

When I first arrived I like many Farangs thought Thailand such a beautifully tolerant society but now I feel that I was mistaken. Travel the Bangkok Sky- Train any day with your Ladyboy lover and you will see the truth. Hold her hand and the staring faces will turn away. Walk by any group of taxi drivers and listen for what they shout, it is not Good day. I punched a Russian man on a baht bus on Christmas day because he thought he could look up Farida's skirt with impunity. He did this in front of his children.

Thais do not blame Ladyboys for their deviance because they believe that karma is the cause of their wrong-genderdness. The academic writing here that emanates from the universities is at once condescending, pragmatic in its search for a 'cure' to the kathoey problem and condemning of their practices. Deriding wrongdoers publicly but taking no action is both historically Thai and confusing to the Westerner. Buddhist writing and creation myths allocate a place to the third gender in the natural order but many consider them objects of pity or ridicule. The absence of gay bashing makes us think that kathoeys are respected members of society. What I see is a family that have little time to even talk to their son/daughter, brother/sister when she returns after a long absence. I see a mother who uses money sent her by her kathoey daughter to give to a poor son who was once a monk. I see family photo albums remarkable for their emptiness of pictures of one child of the family. It is as if Farida never existed. She showed me her photo album of photos of herself and her 'evolution' as a Ladyboy. It was touching and challenging to my perception of her. It was such a cultural and emotional shock but shed such a lot of light on her life I cannot flinch . . . . . I love her more and more . . .

The small children playing by the lake here have raised my spirits today. They smile and say hello. They are beautiful and free from judgment. Farida is so filled with guilt that she feels for disappointing her family because she is a Ladyboy that she will sell herself to earn enough money to pay them. She has worked these past weeks while I have been in Vietnam and saved all the money to splash out here in Surin on presents, party treats and food for the whole neighbourhood come New Years Eve. Buying respectability. She will fail but cannot see it.

I hope she never does. Pity me, because I can.

She has no network of Ladyboy friends, she works alone. Thinks for herself. She is 24 years old. I have never been sure of her love or of how she views me. She has never had a boyfriend and only two customers who spent more than a short time with her. She remembers them and the two or three days she spent in their company. We have been lovers for 3 months now. I have not always been exclusive in my relationship with her but for the last 6 weeks, 'almost' entirely. In my heart, there has only been room for her since we met.

So much can be misinterpreted or lost in an inter-cultural relationship it is difficult to know what is real. I told her that whatever I have I would share with her. It is not enough. I earn 30,000baht a month at the moment, I am asking her to trade on the future. I say that Love may mean change and sometimes sacrifice and I am ready to make that change. She says she cannot eat Love.

I sometimes doubt what I say.

This girl has been my best friend in Thailand, adviser, escort, assistant, and interpreter. She has helped me in every way. Never asking for money when she has done so. I have spent some of the best times I can remember on day trips with her but the nights can be complicated. She saw some photos of other girls, Ladyboys on my phone a few days ago. They were mostly from the past but she was so hurt it made me realise that she loves me. She tells me that she will never answer the question, 'Do you love me?' She admits that if she says this she thinks I will walk away. All this based on pre-adolescent experiences. Maybe I should let her keep working? Before I left for Vietnam she spent every day with me and 'went to working' as she says almost every night. Sometimes she had customers, sometimes not but every night she came to me wherever I was, calling me at 2am and then staying the night. I was always glad to see her. Is it possible for a relationship to work under these circumstances? We made a plan tonight for our return to Bangkok. A business and relationship plan about the nitty gritty of money, trust and the future.

Seven

A change has come; the weather here in Surin is cool and light with warm breezes blowing off the lake. It is New Years Eve and the day has started well. Farida is cooking chicken for tonight's party while wearing a sexy little denim skirt. Yesterday began badly, I was feeling bored and restless probably because being a man-like a child, I want and demand constant attention of the erotic kind. Kissing, touching and hugging keep me and my id happy. Of course this is all in opposition to Thai culture in which even the most ardent of lovers keep their hands in their pockets.

'I understand farang culture' says my darling. 'Good, glad to hear it', says I. Just don't understand it too much, I think.

I had pretty much convinced myself I was going home today alone. The night before we had a conversation in which I had laid out my financial position and what I wanted, asking her if she felt the same and wanted to try making a life together when we get back to Bangkok.

After a lot of repetition on my part and 'alanas' on hers she agreed that she wanted to change her life and mine. I had the sneaking suspicion that she said this to stop me from talking!

Maybe we farangs all forget that even the most seemingly fluent English speaking Thai Ladyboys use up a lot of effort in understanding exactly what we mean. Translating in one's head is hard work and headache inducing especially if the subject is complicated and carries emotional weight.

With this on my mind, I spend the morning reading while she fussed around with make-up and cleaning up after the family. She is the only person I have seen doing any housework since I have been here.

Farida is reading over my shoulder now, she is fascinated by what I write and I think a little bit jealous! But agrees I can carry on writing. She came out to the seat in the garden where I was sitting and sensing something was wrong, asked me, as she does,' What you want to ask me?' I said, nothing. I am done with talking now. You understand what I want and what I feel. My heart is an open book to you but I still don't understand what you want from me. 'I want a rich boyfriend', she says. 'Ok, then I will catch the bus back to Bangkok tonight, because that's not me. No point my staying here just to prolong the agony, better to face the pain on the long ride back to Bangkok, throw my heart out of the window and grow a new one. I was fighting to hold back tears now and failing.

It is not necessary to pay so highly for sex in Bangkok, or in fact necessary to pay at all. I told her so. I told her sex is easy to find but love a lot more difficult.

'If I go back to working, you not see me more?' No. When you are working do you think I will sit in my apartment and wait for you? If I were out fucking other people would you wait at home for me and be happy? 'No', she says. Ok, then, you understand. 'Yes, I understand, we can try, I not go to working more'. Still, the tears were running down my face and then she put her arms around me and we hugged each other for a long time.

Eight

New Years Eve, and just like Christmas this is a polarising event in the calendar. Happy or sad, no middle ground. When were you last really happy on one such day? Back in England the happy holidays were few and far between. Even when my sons were small Christmas, despite having high points, was an event to be 'got through'.

Back there the TV screen shunts out its endless message for the 'republic of desire'; buy this and you will be a better, happier, more desirable person. While selling the Promised land, like Jesus who said 'none shall get to the Father except through me', the advertisers insist that we will only get to that promised land of social acceptance, love and respect through the purchase of their products. We cannot avoid the media in ChickenTown it is as easy to avoid the weather. TV pervades every part of our lives like a crawling mist, like the luminous flesh of a Gibsonian giant, there is no escape.

But here I feel I am blessed. Farida has made Christmas and New Year highs that I won't forget. Every day in this beautiful country is exciting, even a trip to the supermarket is an adventure.

On Christmas Day we spent the morning shopping for Ladyboy size shoes in Pattaya Central Mall. That was not so bad. Then with a brief interlude to visit The Robin Hood and the owner Dave and eat some Christmas food we spent the day and night on Jomtien beach.

Farida was more relaxed than I have known before. We swam, even though she was worried about people seeing her 'pussy' through her little bikini. We ate prawns and papaya salad; it was a piece of heaven. As the sun set we changed at the 500bht hotel room we had booked at 'The Inner Circle' and sank a few drinks before she said, 'let's go back on the beach'. We took some drinks and snacks down to the top end of the beach and spent the night listening to the waves and laughing, lighting fireworks and setting off the 'wish balloons' on their journey to the moon. Magical and Priceless. This kind of happiness, of 'Sabai-jai', cannot be bought.

We were in Surin city, her home for the New Year.

'Shopping, Shopping, Shopping', she says in her artless way and off we go to the market. Sitting behind her on her scooter is a pleasure she does not know I cherish! One arm around her waist, my hand on her stomach and her bum pressed against my crotch is definitely my preferred mode of transport.

The market is full of the sights and sounds that make Thailand so engaging. She does not understand why I take photos on this visit. She is concerned only to buy the food necessary to make the evenings celebration go well. We prepare, or rather she prepares and I get in the way a bit. We eat outside under the trees in the garden. A woman calls who has a beautiful little daughter. The children here are generally so lovely it makes me miss the days when my own sons were small until I remember the struggle I had to raise them alone in the endless dark of British wintertime.

Farida's brother and sister-in-law spend a long time talking with her about their mutual nephew who is 16 and lives with her mum. He is lazy and does not work hard at college. Although I cannot understand their words, the attitude of their hands and faces as they speak remind me that what troubles the Englishman also troubles the Thai and the concerns of modern mankind also occupied the mind of the Saxon, the Roman and those who went before and whose bones have been a long time in the ground.

Friends arrive and tell me all about Liverpool Football club until I tell them I am a Birmingham City supporter. I am getting drunk when the fireworks begin to be set off. I take photos of Farida with her dad. There is something not quite right in that relationship. She has so much need for something, anything from him. He has so much need for her money and asks her openly for it. Comes back later drunk and heedless. Tonight I am everybody's friend and some of them ask me what I feel about Farida. I tell them I love her, tell her, 'Chan rak kuhn', and they shake my hand, drink more whisky, laugh and when we get home even though she has been with me all night she has sent me an SMS message, 'Happy new yrs 2011! thx for come here with me. Wish u happy forever'. My cup overflows.

Nine

The villagers in paradise are not pulling their weight.

The cultural differences make some interactions fraught with possible misinterpretation.

When in a sexual relationship we are so tuned in to each other that a 'look' not returned or a 'look' that seems to say something we don't understand can trigger a bout of ethnic cleansing, or maybe I am too volatile?

Physical contact is an important part of any relationship. Some people are more tactile than others and cultural custom also affects an individual's disposition toward 'touching'. I noticed that Thai people touch each other very little, even if they are closely related. Hugging and kissing siblings, parents and children is non-existent, at least in my limited experience. I cannot imagine a parent in the West coming home from work and not immediately hugging and kissing their small child yet this seems to be the norm in Thailand.

Like a true imperialists I am foisting my western ways onto these people as some kind of improvement, at least those I have contact with. They soon learn enough of our behaviours to appease us I guess. A different matter when the charade that we see enacted in any bar in Bangkok is dropped. Thai's do not interact physically all the time like we do. They 'feel' but do not necessarily 'act' on those feelings all the time. Or maybe it's just me? I am a tactile person and in love even more so. I am always looking for those little things: a look, a smile, a kiss, a hug. Relationships have, for me, always taken place under the Sword of Damocles. My arrogance has a narrative running through my brain that is saying, 'Give in to me, and give me the love and sex I need, when I want it or I walk away'.

Alongside this voice is a second voice saying, Give in to me, give me the love and sex I need, when I want it and I will walk away'.

The first is motivated by the sense of my own importance, of myself as the centre of any known universe, as a jealous god that must be appeased. That appeasement can be made only by a dedicated worship of the mighty cock. Sacrifices must be made by the village women. Virgins must be deflowered and sexual pleasure given unstintingly or the god will be angry. Woe betide the person who tries to withhold sexual pleasure from the god as punishment for a misdemeanour of some kind or a futile attempt at manipulation. For they will be cast into the fiery furnace for all eternity. Ask my ex-wives.

Such has been my relationship history. Give me what I need or I will walk away. But wait, If only it were as simple as that!

The second rune of my libido goes something like: if I can have what I want whenever I want it, then I will plunder your resources like a colonial mine owner and when you are dry; you guessed it, I will walk away. In those kinds of relationships I have actually counted down the days until I am bored, dreading the feeling of emptiness that I know must come.

And so I find myself here laying next to my nemesis; this most gorgeous LB whom I have pursued, courted, loved and cherished but feeling the jealous godhead rising because she won't give me what I want when I want it. I wanted it three times last night, and not once was it granted! Fucking outrageous you say! True! It's too noisy to have sex in this little room with the family only a breath away, she says later. At the time I am not appeased and get up early and take a vengeful walk at 08.15 just to punish her. She was waiting for me when I came back and in her calm way without really speaking made me se how foolish I am. A child.

We broke the bed on the second night here and I was amused at her embarrassment when her brother had to buy a new sheet of plywood (luxury) and her father had to cut it to fit. (400baht) She told me with some shame I think that, 'they know what we have been doing'. I thought it was funny but then I am probably a twat. An arrogant twat who does not really understand Thai interfamilial tensions, particularly where ladyboys are concerned.

Some day soon I must grow up.

Ten

You are running in nighttimes' chirruping heat. Sweat is burning your eyes now and you turn from the dark of soi 6 where you both live onto KrugThonburi Road, alive with pink and yellow taxis, tuk-tuks and the smell of burnt carbon. You thought you could handle her proposition but later a kind of panic gripped your heart and still you cannot breath, but you keep running . . . time is running out.

It is 10.40 as you jump onto the train bound for Bearing. The cold air hits you and you force yourself to sit down. You try to phone her again but again there is no answer. She is doing what she feels she must. Is she doing it for both of you? You have to stop her before it's too late, before the world unhinges itself and all the pieces fly apart destroying everything you love.

A young, pretty girl covered in tattoos sits opposite you: there is only one place she is heading. Just like you. She looks in your eyes and a feeling passes between you, the kind of feeling shared between soldiers moments before a battle. 'Naanaaaa'says the voice of the train. Somebody laughs, somebody always laughs. In the laughter is a kind of nervousness and an edgy, tense excitement.

You wait until the door opens before you leap up and out. Tonight you cannot face the stares of the farang couples on the train. That look that says, 'we know where you are going, and why'. You know that if you see that superior, self- righteousness on the face of a backpacker or a farang woman that something dark and terrible will rise up from inside you and . . . .if they knew what was in your heart they would not stare. Not tonight.

Down the steps to the street you go and into Sukhumvit City. Tourists who should have stayed on Khao San road move toward you blocking the way so you run into the road, a blaring horn shaves so close you feel the wind and suddenly your legs are weak and for the second time tonight you realise that this is really happening, this is not a story. You have to stop her before the unthinkable. You feel like you are moving in slow motion.11.10, and then you are there and you duck under the last awning before the corner and try to push through the throng in the narrow section into the mouth of Nana, soi 4.

Amongst a group of tall Ladyboys you see her. They look for a moment like a team of athletes warming up before an international event, swapping stories of races run and iniquities of life at the sharp end of physical endurance.

For a moment you pause and breathe in. You simply look at her with all the awe and warmth that comes with loving someone. Then you see the white dress the fabulous breasts and beautiful make-up mask and you want her. You move forward and she sees you. She smiles and laughs at you, says your name, 'Ah, Dawid . . .what you do?'

You cannot breathe again. You touch her smooth arms and hold on to her tight because everything is speeding up now. The faces of the other ladyboys follow you as you walk away with your prize. They do not understand. They know you are not a customer because you are crying. Her body is hot like a furnace, she says, let's get some drinks and go home.

In the 7/11 she speaks to another ladyboy, 'This is him' she says. The other ladyboy smiles . . .a broken, ragged smile as if she knows something that you don't.

She walks to the counter with the bottle of Sprite, you hand her 100 baht and two enormous whoremongers who were waiting say, 'They just push right to the front don't they'. You are not sure if they mean Ladyboys, Prostitutes or Thais.

In the cab you look at her face again and you want her, in the worst way a man can want a Ladyboy. Her lipstick is 'fuck-me red' and you play your dirtiest arse-fucking video through one time in your head. You and she are the stars of the show.

In the apartment she gets into bed and says, 'Sleep now', very tired'. You cannot sleep. You want her, want her like any customer could have had her for 1000baht. You have saved her, how can this happen, this is not in the story. In the story you fuck with passion and love and fall asleep together. Something is wrong with the story.

And then what has been locked inside you since you saw her online chat profile, since the first time a customer called when she was with you, since you walked like a zombie from soi to soi while she worked . . .back in September, when you sat outside the Beer Bar in soi 7 and tried to calculate Bangkok, Love and Her in the same equation and failed, is rising like black bile burning your throat and spitting out its poisonous graffiti across the room; the walls, the bed . . . you cannot stop, the floor, her body, you are saying things you do not mean or remember ever having ever thought and you are telling her to get out, you are crying and spitting so much you cannot see or speak any longer. She runs down the passage to the door and you pace behind her shouting, telling her to go, she can sleep in her own apartment. You are stalking towards her now . . .and then she turns to face you and cries, ' I not understand, you come to stop me working at Nana and now you want be like a customer!'

You open your mouth to speak and the devil flies out . . . She is crying so hard her body shakes. The person you swore to yourself you would never hurt is crying. You have never seen her sob before.

You try to hold her and tell her you are sorry . . .and like a drunk driver suddenly sober at the death scene he has caused . . .you see what you have done. She lets you hold her. She is sobbing but says,' Dawid I miss my family much'.

You know that no words you can ever, ever say can bring this moment back.

In the morning she leaves, there are no words that either of you can fit to that moment. It cannot be framed. She leaves behind the key card you gave her only yesterday.

You ride the boat from Pratunam that morning and only one other farang is on this boat and he does not speak or smile. His face is expressionless, seamed with the lines of experience. He sits at the back of the boat and before it is far past Wireless Road he reaches inside his overcoat and seeming to struggle with something inside his clothing, at his breast, he pulls out something black and hard and looking around the boat, tosses it over the side. He smiles a sigh of relief as if to say, 'See how easily that was done'. He gets off at the next dock and you watch him walk away, lightness in his step.

In Bangkapi Mall the record store is playing country and western

music and as you walk past, Johnny Cash floats through the speakers. It feels like a cruel joke as you remember the words: 'Come sit down beside me and hear my sad story,
For I'm shot in the breast, And know I must die'.

You call her as you leave for home, no answer, no answer, no answer, Then you are there at her apartment hammering at the door almost out of control until you hear her shout, 'Ai' from her shower . . . .she opens the door wearing a towel and shower cap. Easier to concentrate on what you must do when she does not look so attractive. You think yourself a bad man for having that thought but push it down and walk inside. Despite all your promises, despite all your rationalisations, despite your education, experience, years of strife, despite your Englishness you find yourself once again begging her not to go back to work, the tears blinding you as you speak.

You tell yourself to be a man, but if you are to face what you know will come, (22.26hrs-06.01.2011-first customer of the night) then you must face it like Macduff and feel it like a man.

She shakes her head when you try to convince her you can both live on 1000baht a day. She knows better and so do you. You have lived through the arguments that a lack of money brings. Your mother used to say, 'when money problems come in the door, love flies out the window!'

But you believe love conquers all don't you. Dreamers like you fuck up the natural order; disrupt the laws of the jungle.

So dreamer that you are you sit by her side and hold her hand as she tells you that despite last nights unforgivable act, you will be forgiven, that she will feel the same/same feelings for you no matter how many customers she has. That even if a rich farang wanted to make her his waan jai, she would not stay with him and that she will be careful and that her heart will always belong to you. You cry, swallow and when she asks you to promise that you will keep the same/same feelings for her, you promise to try. You promise because you know that you cannot live without her in your life. She tells you that it may not be for long, if you find a job with good money.

Money is evil, you say. She likes shopping and asks if you will buy her old television set from her for your sad and empty room along the street because she wants a new one with a big screen. You remember watching her father using the scrap wood from her broken bed to patch his only window. When you go back to your room alone, on your bed is a single false eyelash.

Eleven

Lonely. Last night I went to look for the right medicine to cure the pain. I found medicine of sorts in Dao on Soi 7/1. She made me forget the heartache for a while but it came back this morning and Farida and I went shopping. Everything was beautiful as it always is when we are together. We had fun,

laughed, loved each other and talked a little. Later we sat in my room drinking and thinking about trying to make love without complications. It soon became clear that although I was very ready and willing, although she was willing she was far from ready. I had told her before that we should only make love when she wants. I stopped short and told her, 'lets just go eat, forget about sex, no problem, ok?

She got very distant because she thought i did not want her although the evidence was to the contrary.

I told her my reasons; I cannot have sex with someone I love when they do not want the same and I do not want to feel like a customer having perfunctory sex as quickly as possible. Not with someone I love. She is in control with customers, her feelings are locked away safe and her body means less than zero to her. Her soul and her heart are simply not there. The money is only really a small part of it. She needs to control her life, her feelings.

We talked about this in detail and yes, I asked her again to stop.

I realised that she picked somewhere close to eat because she wanted to go to work at 9.30. She gave me just a little of her time tonight.

Before we parted I told her I loved her but cannot be with someone who does not put me before the purchase of a new television and new clothes. We stood in Soi 6 and she begged me not to say goodbye. It was heartbreaking but my heart had already broken, yesterday. I told her that someone else wanted to be with me and did not care about money and she was coming from Pattaya to stay with me for a week. I told her I would not do this if she gave up working. We were both crying by now. I told her I loved her but cannot take the pain of knowing she is fucking other men. I told her we could work it out, all the sex stuff, because I love what is inside of her.

She called a passing motorcycle and climbed on the back. I will never forget her face as she drove away from me for the last time. She called me half an hour later and asked me why I said goodbye to her. I don't think she believed I was serious, but I knew what I had to do and so last night I made something die in my heart. I have no more tears left to cry. Later I went to Nana and she was there. I told her that she had made her choice but I loved her and that when she chose to stop working even in 5 years from now, I would be waiting.

But for now I am going to try and build something good between Oh and me. Oh is a ladyboy I met just after I met Farida and our chemistry was great immediately. I took it no further then because I was loyal to Farida. Maybe we can make each other happy?

Twelve

DAWID! DAWID, OPEN THE DOOR I WAN TALK WID YOU!
Blood freezes. Oh's shocked eyes scare me even more. We are naked and wet.

DAWID! DAWID, OPEN THE DOOR I WAN TALK WID YOU!
I was putting my heart and head back together after my world with Farida fell apart. Oh was helping me. I was swallowing her good medicine.

I shouted through the door for her to wait, she was not going to leave. Her voice; jagged and brittle, ready to break.

She should not have been able to get upstairs past the security door. She must have waited for someone who knew us to let her in. I stepped into the hallway.

She said in broken English and with a breaking tremor in her voice, 'she in there, you busy'? I led her away from the room thinking déjà-vu. Been here before and I didn't like it the first time. The temptation to run away and leave them to it vanished when I looked in Farida's face.

We sat on a faux leather armchair in the farang friendly reception area and she did the strangest thing. She slapped me on the leg with both hands and said, 'We go eat prawns at Raemkampang road Dawid', let's go, ok!' Then her face contracted like a muscle in shrink-wrap. My heart broke all over again. I needed time to let go of her and she had not given it to me. She had tipped me off balance again.

I said, 'You threw me away when you went back to working, why you come here now?' She said, 'No, No, I have same, same feeling. 'I not go to working more Dawid'!

'Really, for sure?'

'Yes, for sure'.

Surprisingly and with horror I realised I felt nothing. Not joy, not happiness, only a concern about what I will say to Oh waiting in the room.

Then all of a sudden it happened, I looked at myself in a way I had been much too fast to do whenever events like these unfolded themselves in my life. This mess was all my fault.

I had known Oh for some time and we really hit it off, she is a truly lovely person. I took our relationship no further because I met Farida. Two days after she went back to work at Nana I called Oh and asked her to come and stay with me for the week. She caught the bus from Pattaya the next morning. It was too soon and now my selfishness and hunger was causing pain to her and Farida. I told Farida that Oh was coming to be with me, their were no lies involved but I just was not careful enough of both their hearts, or mine. What now?

I told Farida I would not send Oh away, that was not the right thing to do. We needed to talk more though. I did not believe that she would stop working just like that, I felt cautious. I told Farida to be sure this is what she wants and to send me an SMS that night if she was 100% ready. then I said, and only then would I talk to Oh.

When I went back into the room Oh was sitting on the balcony quietly smoking. I sat down opposite her and a single tear rolled down her pretty face. A tough thing to see on such a pretty face. 'This always happen to me', she said, 'Someone throw me away'.

I told her that was not true. What could I say? I told her the truth.

I made sure I looked after her well that afternoon and her spirits rose when I took her out. She wanted to see Nana Plaza and Asoke so she dressed like a working girl. 'I try on clothes for wear tonight and you say ok or not'! What a girl! She was making me smile again. Then I got the message from Farida,

'Ok am stop work Ic u tomorrow n hv a good dream!'

Difficult to remember how I felt.

Oh and I did the tour of Nana and Asoke street bars and went to eat a great papaya salad on Soi 7. Then I told Oh we could go back to Nana and see if Farida had really stopped.

I left Oh in Big Dog and walked along the street and there she was! This time, no begging, no complaining. I told her if she did not go home now I would never speak with her again, even as a friend. I do not like lies. She said' why I just to go home my room alone when you with she'? I said 'Well maybe you will understand what it was like for me when you were working before?' I collected Oh and left. I told her that I had asked her to come and be with me too soon and that she should go back to Pattaya in the morning while I decided what to do. Bless her, she did not argue and promised to wait until I could think straight. Her behaviour during this horrible episode was so graceful and gentle that she deserves only the best. If I can I will give it to her. A new pair of breasts perhaps.

Karma was at work here because the day after she got back her mum was taken ill, dementia, I think and Oh and her sister had to take her home to Buriram.

Farida took a taxi home after I left that night. Not sure if she had any customers but I decided I don't care. She deserves a chance even if it's a chance to hang herself. So now we live on 1000baht a day, I go to work most days and she sleeps, eats and shops, and chats online. She is a compulsive online chatter, child that she is, so if she has promised you that she is looking for a serious relationship, don't hold your breath, or send her money!

Fooling around with her yesterday, just being silly and laughing in the taxi from Chinatown reminded me again just why I love this girl. She makes me feel good when we are together and what happens between us seems so intimate. She feels like my best friend. I began to fall in love with her all over again, then when I came home tonight at 7.30 she had painted her nails, put on make up and I knew she was going to work again. I had bought her three red roses from Pratunam, they will die soon.

We went to eat and I told her I would be her friend, everything the same, same but no sex or boyfriend/girlfriend stuff. Maybe we will have a business together; she's a tough girl, useful to have around.

I cannot cry any more over her. I cannot do it. I told her I cared for her but could not get hurt again and so cannot be her boyfriend. She said, 'but I know you love me'. I said, 'are you, are you really sure?' Something has changed in me and she saw it, I saw her see it and she changed too.

She told me that if I cannot take care of her, as she would wish, what **can** I do for her? I asked her the same question . . . can she love me, be my trusted friend and adviser and fuck me with passion at least once a day? I think the absolute minimum requirement for a girlfriend in Thailand.

Once before she had told me, 'yes' but had failed on at least two counts. 'Well, can you?' Once before, when we met you told me that money was first for you, before love, happiness, sex, now it's time to change. Because if you will not, then I have no interest in talking further with you. I can make one phone call and replace you tomorrow with someone who does not want or ask for money, only love (she knows I can do this) If you cannot tell me now, right now, then goodbye!' She looked me right in the eyes and said, 'Ok, I will try to do all you want for 7 days, but if I no can do it what then, throw me away?'

The tables had turned. I remembered who I am. I don't need her. Today. I will wait to see what tomorrow brings.

Thirteen

Putting it All to Rest

Her long back and round bottom are spread before you like the landscape of home. You are deep in the southern countryside. It is hot and wet down there like the jungle and you are penetrating deeper than you have ever been before. The passage is narrow and she screams as you use more force to widen the way. It feels senseless and simple and raw and you need it so badly after the vacillating relationships twists and turns of the week gone by.

She has been to Nana again, not for customers, she says but to talk business with her friend, but still she took the Ladyboy survival kit: condoms x 6, lotion x 1, kamagra gel x 2 as she can rarely get hard without it. Too many hormones, vitamin supplements and bad customers.

But for now, that's forgotten; she has told you again that she wants to be your girlfriend and all that it entails. You have your doubts and keep them hidden most of the time. At 3 am last night she woke you up. 'Dawidd, lets go to the Night market, ok?' 'Ok, you say and then walk around Chinatown for an hour in which she is all yours, she holds your hand fiercely, protectively; the looks and the cat-calls do not trouble her, she walks like a sexy queen, on oriental princess amongst Bangkok's unwashed.

You sit together on a step as the early hours open around you. She tells you that you think too much about sex. To her it is a job and unlike most Thai's she can be as closed as a fist. She says she will try to be different with you. Today she did just that and the world became a better place for a while. You explain to her that all you ask is that the intimacy you share when you are together continues and deepens when you make love. You say that the biggest turn-on in sex is nothing to do with what she wears or her make-up but that she lets you inside and looks in your eyes with love and passion. You say you understand that this will take time. Secretly you think this is a tall order but true love is demanding.

After you make love you lay together half waking and asleep. You feel happier than you remember for a long time. You know it won't last.

You plan to eat prawns and now you will do anything for her, spend any amount of money if you can, but you have 400 baht left for the day. She has spent the 500baht you gave her this morning at the market. You go home to find more money and agree to meet her in a few minutes, you live so close but the time slips by you; an email or two, a beer and she is calling you, mad. You go to her room and a darkness has clouded her face. You leave for Ekamai anyway but you tell her, 'just half an hour, that's how long I was'! On the Sky-Train you tell her she is reminding you of Farang women who nag and that you came to Bangkok to escape that kind of existence. Watching the clock is necessary when you are working but not now, not tonight, who cares where you go and what you do as long as you are together? She is obdurate and says, 'Sure, you can do what you want, and so can I!' Your mind is beginning to boil but you will not argue, that reminds you too much of England and the relationships you left behind. You love her, that much is true but can you bear this, this mood that you think speaks of something more than being kept waiting? You cannot. But you do not know what to do. You have forgotten how to say 'No'. Love has robbed you of something, but your body has not forgotten. As the Sky train pulls into Nana, the doors open and your body steps off onto the platform.

You do not look back as you walk into your new Bangkok.

On the platform you watch a mechanical digger pick up earth in its giant dinosaur-like mouth and swinging its great arm through 180 degrees dump the soil into the back of a waiting truck. You watch it for a long time; scoop, swing, empty, over and over again. Nothing good lasts forever.

Fourteen

Learning the meaning of 'coming to an end' is a bitter business. Stupidly, painfully you are getting it by heart that any talk, any quarrel, any kindness you have shared with her will never be resolved, never finished if you live to be eighty years old. The thread between you has been snapped. An End. Never. These words that have been only sounds before grow big and dwarf you.

You struggle through each day as if imprisoned in a long, dark tunnel. Yes, you have gained wisdom, though not too much from the events of the last few months.

You will try hard not to give in to sadness without a fight, you will try hard to be content with your lot. This is how it will be.

All the time your loneliness and desire for her, starved as it is, will grow as thin as a razor blade that will dig into your heart so deep that you will feel that it will be sliced in two. This is how it will be for you dreamer as predicted by the laws of logic, good sense and as written into the book entitled, 'On loving prostitutes'.

But dreamer, you wanted the moon and everyone knows the moon cannot be had. You tried, you did not stay on the ground looking up at her and wishing. You climbed the tallest building and you jumped and fell. But at least you tried.

You cannot say the final goodbye that you know you must take and part ways. She is sitting on a red plastic stool barring your way down the small soi leading from the Sky-Train to her apartment. You are surprised she is there waiting to eat.

She asks if you can sit and eat with her, as if she were something poisonous. You think of what you said last night in the street, shouting so loud and screaming that a crowd gathered to watch the Farang and Ladyboy prostitute that share their apartment block fighting and you are filled with shame.

You ask if she is ok now. She says she is sad, so sad and cannot cry now. Her lips are swollen. She says now she knows 'nothing can do and so I say myself, nothing can do and now I stop from crying'.

You think, how like Farida this is. She may be only a scrap that last night you threw into the raging seas, but she is a scrap of cork.

You want to know if you were ever special to her, you touch her heart. 'Was it true, or all lies, was I special in your heart?'

'I know you love me', she says. Was I special to you! 'Oh Dawid' she says, I meet you in Nana, I am a prostitute, you know this', it not matter now, why you ask wid me?'

'I want to think GOOD of you', you burst out, 'not to believe you would lie to me . . .Farida, don't look away; please, don't look away. Your voice thickens and you break off, humiliated. What a stupid animal you are, afraid now to look at her so you might hold in the tears. When you look at her at last, forcing yourself. You see her eyes wide and glistening and beautiful. Your beautiful girl. 'Nobody speak wid me like you' she said. 'I won't do it again' you say. 'Nobody ever think me good,' her mouth trembled, 'nobody, never'.

Tears run down her cheeks. She grabs a handful of toilet roll napkin from the table and holds it against her face. She is crying so fiercely that her body shakes. Minutes later she says, 'If I say I love you, I am scared Dawid, my heart break'. She holds onto your shoulders and into your ear she whispers, those words that only a child can use without understanding the human weight they carry, 'I love you Dawid'

For two years she had lived under blows, curses and been used like an animal. An animal can only be punished but a human spirit can be shamed and appealed to. You had wanted to think good things about her. You had spoken to her soul.

You sit together as the food shops close down and the streetlights fade, the small passage becoming a cocoon in which you wait for the strength to move on with your lives alone.

We held hands, and spent that time not in lust or anger but in a mutual forgiveness and tenderness.

I was simultaneously a man who had at last come home and a man who must go away forever.

After that night we could be nothing to one another. I must reconcile myself with this.

I prepared to leave her, opening a wound in myself that I know will never quite heal. There was nothing to be gained in spinning out our parting. It would hurt just as much when the moment came but I could not leave just yet. We sat longer, not talking but in some kind of peace. At the entrance to her apartment, I held onto her for one last time and kissed her so tenderly. One minute we were there under a weak yellow street lamp, a motorcycle taxi driver yawning in the passageway; ' happy, live happy' she said. She held out her hands to me and I clasped them. I gazed at her, my darling, upright and beautifully strong as a cherry tree in blossom and with as little need of me.

The next minute, we turned away, crunching the midnight gravel under our shoes and Farida Boonjue went out of my life.

Fifteen

You fell asleep at 5am so when his voice 'Hallo Mr Dawid' wakes you it feels as though you are being dragged from the mud and slime at the bottom of a very deep well.

'I want to talk wid u, I see your pwofile, Because of your state he has taken the opportunity to speak before you ask, 'Who the fuck are you, and what do you want?"

'Faybook, see you number'. 'Sorry but I am only interested in ladyboys'!

'I have two ladyboys I want u meet', now an eyelid flickers, 'They are twins', now you are coming awake!

'Why you want me to meet them? You their boyfriend?' 'No no no kun David, I am gay man!'

So why you want me to meet twin ladyboy prostitutes? 'They not prostitute, they student, before, you know, before, I their teacher!'

You did not expect that! They want to have farang boyfriend so can speak English better.

Mmmmnnn, you think. Something reptilian is stirring in your consciousness but you do not trust Thai men. What's in it for him?

Noting, I only tink they goood girls na, want them speak little better English. More prudent men would have let things lie.

You called the number he gave you and a voice from the other side of sleep greeted you in slurred Thai.

Definitely a bar girl! Asleep at 2pm. Having only just awoken yourself you feel you are perfectly placed to judge the moral turpitude of late risers in Bangkok.

'She only have day off', Wasit, for that is his name, assures you.

You agree to meet Ice at 5pm near Sala Daeng BTS. You tell a friend you are going.

She is tall, slim and so clearly not a working Ladyboy that you are relieved but almost simultaneously bored.

Quite what Wasit has been teaching her is unclear as she does not speak more than 5 words of English. For the first time in months you feel linguistically superior. You speak at least 6 words in Thai.

You agree to meet her sister the next day and also plan to meet a beautiful Thai Ladyboy whom you have decided will be your next waan jai. (sweetheart)

Life is beginning to taste a little sweeter and you follow a leggy chick up the stairs at Siam station, cock twitching in your pants as you think about that feeling when a smooth thigh slips between your hairy ones and massages your cock . . . the IPod is playing your theme tune:

I am your main man if you're looking for trouble I'll take no lip 'cause no ones tougher than me If I kicked your face you'd soon be seeing double Hey little girl, keep your hands off me 'cause I'm a rocker I'm a rocker!

You realise you are singing out loud and only stop yourself from punching the air because you're not drunk, yet!

Drinking is delayed because the twins are 1 hour late. Fuck this! Waiting at Siam is like a living death.

Farang tourists are shopping at what is perhaps the most sophisticated mall in Thailand and points west but you see more ethnic beads, striped calico hippy shirts and fisherman's trousers than you have ever seen on Khao San road! Fuck me, you think, where do they think they are, the jungle?

You have arranged to meet Fon at 7pm so when they arrive at 6.37 you buy them ice cream and leave. You will never see them again. If you live here for 40 years you are sure that there are some things you will never understand about Bangkok!

Fon is Batgirl. One look at her thigh muscles has you. She strides masterfully by your side like a muscular Doberman bitch. Her smile is sweet and you tell her you would like to bottle it. 'No can do' she says, flirting ever so slightly. You have a hard on so don't remember the best things she said. You go to a party at Ratchada with her team from the bank where she works. Heaven. Her co-workers are: a busty ladyboy, a tall, dark ladyboy with a killer smile that she directs at you from under her fringe, (You have a hard on so cannot remember anything she said.) and several gay men. Oh, yes and one plump woman but you don't really notice her because, yes, you have a hard on. Fon presses her ass into your crotch and dances like an athlete. She reminds you of a body-builder. There is a show which comprises gay boys dancing in skimpy clothes but you don't have a hard on so cannot remember what else they did. You buy a bottle of whisky and everyone thinks you are a great fellow. A high price to pay for popularity you think: 1000baht. You think yourself a cheap Charlie and smile. Fon is putting her strong hands under your clothes. Fucking hell, not for the first time you feel like a girl, the hunted, not the hunter! Wowwww, you wonder if you like this? Moments later you answer yourself in the affirmative because now you have a hard on. For a 'good girl' Fon is Superbad!

You leave the club at 3am because you have to get up for work at 7.30 so you try to be conservative but when you are going home you get a message from Neung aka Anna, a sexy red-headed minx of a ladyboy who distributes her brand of love, laughter and bonhomie from Nana

4 to soi 11 and the Offstation Bar. First time you met her she was patrolling Nana, a spot you know only too well. Neung insisted you take her back to Thonburi and insisted you fuck her and then insisted you take pictures of her. She is a big insister. She makes you laugh so much you spit coke over the floor and you feel good.

This girl fucks like an oiled up otter. A really dirty little fuck with an innocent looking face is worth having and so I did. She is a really sexy, funny LB. She enjoys what she does and loves the attention.

The next night it is Fon again and this is the 4th date! She has small but rock hard tits and when you hold her hand as you walk they rub against your arm and prevent any kind of rational thought.

You get a cab from Silom and go back to your place. Once there she lies back on your bed while you strip her down. 'Not so Superbad now little girl', you think, pleased with your big, bad self! You are disappointed to find she has no tits! How did; what happened to them? Her body is laying out beneath you now and you pull of your clothes and take down her panties. She has a big hard cock. She takes hormones only rarely. You suck it and she lies there like Cleopatra. Her cum tastes sweet and she sighs with pleasure.

But now it is arse-fucking time; in my experience a moment when a look of anxiety often crosses a Ladyboys face. You are remorseless. She must pay for her beauty and you are the collector of the gorgeousness tax. You take your duty seriously despite the effort and sweat it demands. She is so glad to finally be paying her dues that after what only seems like 10 minutes her beautiful brow puckers and she begins to say, then scream in your face, come, come, COME!!!!! Duty observed, you oblige the lady and she screams one last time as you plunge in to the hilt before she breathes again.

What follows is what always follows, the Ladyboy two step. One step off the bed, the second step that starts the dash to the toilet. The door shuts and an enormous farting shit ensues behind it. Ahhhh, music to your ears. She comes back with a smile but dresses quickly as she has to work on the morrow. You notice she is brief in her goodbyes and refuses to allow you to accompany her to the end of the soi and taxi rank. She assures you she can find her way and 'call me tomorrows' you.

When you go back into the apartment the stench hits you. You have grown accustomed to the post sex ladyboy shit smell but this is something else. The toilet looks like you imagine Calcutta on a bad day. Shit is splattered in and on the toilet itself. The floor and wall is coated as well. You have no equipment for cleaning. You master your senses and kneel to commit the final act of Ladyboy worship that night. You clean up her shit with a hose and your hands.

The following night you are not surprised when she does not answer your calls. Such is life. Such is shit and its capacity for embarrassment.

Sixteen

Clearing all traces of her from your life is difficult. Things creep up on you unexpectedly. Drunk, you search for the only cup you posses and find it in the bathroom. She liked to use it to clean her teeth. Memory is a harsh realm.

Drunk you download her video from Ladyboy 69 and masturbate bitterly as she shoots her load. Together in ejaculation. Sad as hell.

Fon is back on the scene but there is something not quite right about this girl. She earns about 12,000baht a month but her apartment costs 5,000 baht. There has to be another source of income. It is not you, that's for sure.

Dishonesty is not appealing. Lies do not need to be told to men like you. Nothing can stop your relentless pursuit of; what is it you are pursuing again? Are you having an existential crisis, are you going to start beginning sentences with phrases like, 'actually I find some aspects of Buddhism appealing '

No, you are not, you are going to fuck the shit out of many Ladyboys and tell everyone about your adventures. That is what you will do. That will be your cure.

Saw her sitting there by the record machine (waiting for the boat at Bangkapi actually) I guess she must have been about 17? The iPod's turned on, playing her song I knew it wouldn't be long before she was with me, yeh me Singing I love Joan Jett and you look just like her! Those newbies who ask the same question time and time again, 'Where can I find Ladyboys'? Answer, everywhere you go in Bangkok!

Looking like Joan Jett in her heyday may present problems for a 17-year-old Ladyboy who looks like she only just grew her hair out but I cannot think of any. I am standing in the sun wearing 'I fuck Ladyboy shades', and I smile ever so slightly at her. She arches her eyebrows even more, puckers her moody, sexy mouth in my direction, lifts her chin and looks to her right. Shameless little bitch. We recognise each other.

A plug and a socket. Cool. I smile more and the other people waiting watch me do it. I look in the eyes of a man and a woman who are staring. They look away. She lifts her chin again in that way that Thais have of saying, Alai? What's up, what you want? Now I know I have her. She smiles.

The boat arrives, I get on and she does not. Now I know where she works. We will meet again. Ladyboys are like men; they just cannot keep it in their pants.

Post Farida and I am thinking about finding a lady, fuck those Ladyboys! I do. On the boat, at immigration, on street, 'Hey beautiful, where you go? Works for the LB's, why not me? Sure enough, they all are going my way baby. Just gotta ask, face possible rejection, (what's rejection say long time Thailand mongers) same, same England, it can happen. Arrange future meetings that night, later, tomorrow with sexy little Jum, sexy little Lin (Burmese student) and sexy little Noy (student and beauty shop owner) Takes place in one day. Don't think, just do is the motto to adopt, bit like a fucked up Nike advert.

Just when I think I am winning, the Vengeful God of Ladyboys decides to intervene; 'finished with us you say! Ha Ha Ha, you fool!'

And she is there and I am making eye contact with such a one as this, a goddess, a queen surrounded by crows on the MRT.

Enter Ladyboy Tan. Oh boy. This story suddenly has balls!

Tan-Meeting 1: Asoke, a street bar. Brief meeting to check out her 'story' before meeting the New Yorker. She tells me she works in marketing earning 5,000baht a month but sometimes meets farangs to boost her income. She says she has worked about 1 night a month at a beer bar in Patpong but has only ever had 4 or 5 customers in a year of working there. Why? I not like work bar she says and FaceBooks me. Fon calls, 'what you do, want to meet me I finish work now'?

Its 6pm, I am walking to the BTS, Farida jumps out on me from behind the steps, 'Dawid, I poot, I poot'. Still touchy about her I walk a few steps up and look down on her. 'What?' Customer, want me poot (poo) on he face and pee pee in him mouth, ha ha ha'. 'Really', I say. 'Sure, only just to coming home'. She had been to a hotel in Sukhumvit with a farang she met on Camfrog. He asked her to shit on him while he lay in the Jacuzzi and piss on his face. Apparently, her turds were a bit hard and he lined them up on the edge of the tub before smearing them on himself. The New Yorker told me it takes 'every kinda people', he is right. He injected her ass with a syringe full of soapy water to make her poo more copiously. She thought it hilarious and could not understand why he paid her 1500baht for her poo.

I said that's nice, smiled and said,' why you tell me? I not care what you do. I don't care Farida, good luck. Her smile vanished. I walked away, smiling to stop the tears from coming again. She sends me a message, 'Can se my face smile not real Come back to me David'

Crying on the Sky train is becoming a bad habit. I wear shades, turn the music up loud.

Tan-Meeting 2: My Loom 11pm, Telephone Convo beforehand; She: I come see u now. I wan see u.

Me: I like to see u too, but cannot pay you. She: Why u no pay.

Me: Not need, have many friends . . . understan? She: I wan come Thonburi, see u . . . now.

Me: Ok, but I no pay you. She: OK, I like u (beat) U pay for taxi me home?

Me: (in the role of Generous George) Sure. See you.

She arrives on long, smooth legs. She has the best looking and feeling bolt-on breasts I have seen on any man, woman or child. She has an asshole like an otter's pocket. She brings her own silicone bodyglide and fucking commences in magnificent style.

Two nights before the glorious Gate of Guess Bar had come over. She lives across Krunthonburi road and I met her the day before getting of the Sky-Train. She looked cute and I was a bit horny so kissed her and invited her over. She did not arrive until 5 hours after the time she said she would! We sat on the floor of my loom and ate, chatted and got to know each other again after the debacle that ensued when she followed me down to Pattaya. She is, was and always will be almightily fucked up. I have a soft spot for her and its not my cock. She told me she had no customers for three days and no one had fucked her for 10 days. If there is one thing Gate likes it is being fucked, because when she is stroking it with a cock up her ass all the shit that goes on in her head disappears. Poor Gate had to pay the price of beauty and fame. On seeing my cock after an absence of some time she told me, 'I little bit scared'. Had her asshole grown over? She was shouting 'come, come, COME', minutes (shamefully few) later. She is such a good fuck I cannot help myself with her! She told me she needs to keep in practice to manage taking a cock up her arse, a layoff can be a bad thing, the work just piles up doesn't it? Tan showed no such fear although a look passed over her face as might be seen on nature programs when the swimming zebra feels the first nip of the crocodile's teeth. It knows what is coming. Tan did not try to out-swim my advances which would have been silly. She took it like the (23 year old) man that she is.

This girl is fucking beautiful! Her body is top-notch. Hormones or not there is nothing limp about Tan. I took a good long time fucking the shit out of her. She loved it. Every position and nuance was fantastic and after I came she climbed astride me pinning me to the bed and said, 'I want to come now', in a husky voice. A first for me, being pinned to the bed! Wow, what a woman! After a few minutes she spurted all over my chest. Fucking hell.

She stayed the night and we rode the Sky train together. She got off at Sala Daeng. I watched those long legs walk away.

Two days later she came to my apartment at 9am. She works at 12.30pm. The same great time was had by both, this time she came while giving her head. She asked me to be her boyfriend for true. 'What's mean?' I said, knowing just like the zebra, what is coming next. 'You take care me'.

Me: I cannot, no money Tan: Have, have! Me: No have Tan: How you have girlfrlend before? Me: She go, cannot take care her (swallowing hard) Tan: Why you no have money?

Me: I can help you, put picture on Ladyboy website. Tan: What?? (I explain) Me: Maybe you meet good man can take care you? Tan: I wan u!!!!!!

Me: No can, no money. You good girl, someone like you sure. Tan: How much can take care me? 5,000 baht one month, I not want much. Me: (that's a great deal, I think) You working as well at marketing job and go with other customer. Tan: Yes but I wan you take care of me, not like customers, not like working bar, want boyfriend. Me: I put pictures on web, you want me to put your telephone number? Tan: Yes ok, and address (she gives me her address in Bang Na) Me: I not put address but men can call you if they want to meet ok.

Tan: Ok, they can call you, you call me. Me: No, they can call you! Tan: I see you tonight? Me: Maybe

Seventeen

Nobody's perfect

Farida comes to say goodbye. She is going to Surin for a few days to see her family. You cannot go; the emotional price is too high.

She throws off the linen cloth she has been wearing to walk up the soi to your apartment.

She is wearing a white tank top and no bra. Her dark nipples and perfect tits have you clutching at her like a drowning man grabbing a sexy looking raft.

You fuck and talk and try not to get sad. Since the night you parted she has not left you alone. She is in your mind every minute and you cannot get her out. She knows this.

You told her that when she gets back from Surin you cannot see her more. 'Too much hurt' you say. She says that she will quit but you have heard that before.

Its not that she is lying, its just that she wants to be with you so much that she cannot say goodbye even though you both know that is what will happen soon.

You have already planned your exit strategy.

'Where you' says a voice from the phone. It is 08.30 am. 'In bed', you say. 'I come see you now'. A beat. 'Ok' says the reptile. 'See u soon'! Strange how once they have been here Ladyboys decide that Thonburi is not so far after all. Lazy little mares.

Later, standing by the photocopier bullshitting with an American colleague is pretty everyday but not in Bangkok and not if you work where I do!! A part time Thai teacher you have spoken with briefly is actually photocopying while you look on. Something is bothering you and you are only, 'aha'ing and uhu'ing' the yank. She has such a pretty face. She is flat chested. She has big feet. Is she? Could she be, here, at work?

As she walks away you watch with undisguised lust, naked lust, lust covered in baby oil and blood.

She is a fucking Ladyboy. Holy shit! You look back at the yank who looks concerned and says in a stage whisper, 'confidentially man, I gotta tell you, that's no chick, that's a man. 'I don't care what she is', you say. 'Ooooo K' says the yank, like they do. 'She's gorgeous', you say, feeling your eyes glaze as you speak.

What a job, what a city, what a fucking complicated mess you could make of your whole life if you don't STOP NOW!

That night Guess Bar is full of lipstick Lucifers dressed as University girls. Gate calls you over to 'her corner' and asks you about taking photos for her and tells you about her webcam exploits. Everything she says drips with a languid, sensual oil that goes so well with her lip gloss. 'When I come over see you 'gain?' 'Whenever you like, just call ok.' You know that you can probably write a fucking book between the time she says she will arrive and the actual time she arrives which could be as much as 6 hours apart. She is the queen of lazy mares. It's the drugs, she is the xanax queen of Bangkok.

She is a rebel though, complaining she doesn't like the uniform even though she looks fantastic. She is forever standing in the mirror undoing her shirt to reveal those terrific tits and then tying it up again. She is hoping you notice and she smiles when she sees you look and makes that funny little half-laugh, half-snort through her nose.

It works and you tell her after you have done the rounds you will call her and share taxi home, etc, etc, etc. She knows you speak with forked tongue.

The New Yorker and Big T are at the bar and you join in. Teasing Cherry, playing with her tight little body is distracting but when Nan makes an entrance the air is sucked out of the room.

You ask the New Yorker to introduce you. He knows everyone, even you. She is tall enough to look right in your eyes. She is fucking magnificent. Now you are leaving, fate plays its hand, or cock, in this case. You need the toilet and as you exit the rear door Cherry walks in front of you and you follow her down the corridor. As you near the toilet Cherry stops and you hear the Guess Bar door open and close behind you. Nan runs down the passage and both she and Cherry push and drag you into the ladies. Fucking hell, is this paradise? Nan has you against the wall and is pushing her tongue down your throat and kissing you in the way that makes you think of a hungry anteater. Cherry has her hand down your trousers.

Another girl walks in but you can only look at Nan's mouth, don't know who, but as quickly as it began the party is over, almost. Nan straightens her dress and you stand together in the corridor kissing for a few moments as she gives you her phone number. It is still only about 10.00pm.

Temptations; and you are, but resist the smooth skinned minx that has put herself in your line of sight since you walked in. Finally you invite her over and like a happy spaniel she hops up next to you.

The New Yorker is besieged by a succession of gorgeous friends. Cascades is like a scene from 70's exploitation movie.

The beautiful, female explorers have been captured by fuck-thirsty natives and have chained them all to a small, rocky island to await the arrival of their' god' to whom they are sacrifices.

The New Yorker and I are jealous gods indeed and we want them all! They must pay the price for their beauty and sacrifice their 'virtue'?

to our desire.

I spot my victims from the back row where a handmaiden is handling me. The other handmaidens and water carriers are paying homage to the New Yorker. He is magnanimous in power, a benevolent god of the waterfall.

The denizens of the cascade are begging, 'Take us all', take us all, we must be punished for our beauty and our vanity and thinking we are glamour models although we can do the walk and everything and I sucked the owner of Fashion TV's nipple in the Majestic suites so I am a sort of model aren't I?'

They say all this telepathically but I promise never a truer word was spoken.

My victims ask if they may dress before leaving with me to meet their doom. Reluctantly I agree as it's a bit chilly outside. I am a benevolent god too.

In the taxi Cyn and Am (there's a joke in there somewhere) for those are their names show me videos on their tiny annoying blackberry's 'what' they made. Mostly they consist of a mirror's eye view as they make faces at the camera.

They tell me about their exploits in various hotels we pass.

Their legs are long and brown and I am sitting in the middle and fondling their bodies, preparing them for the sacrifice to come.

I have decided I will use a dagger on each of them or maybe a sword? Yes, a sword made of meat.

In the loom, they take showers and Cyn comes out first so we begin kissing and stroking. I am tempted to impale her then and put her out of her obvious misery, but sheath my sword temporarily as Am joins in.

Kissing one, being blown and stroked by the other is pretty much heaven.

Am's body is slim and her tits look big and beautiful.

Cyn is browner, bigger and her cock is long and sickle shaped for fucking around corners.

I am sucking Am's cock and Cyn asks if she can fuck me? 'You like I fuck you?'

Never having experienced that, I agree but with the rider that she stop if I not like. 'Ok' says the Amazon and gets a lot of jelly and cream out, oh, and a condom.

She looks as if she is preparing for a deep-sea dive or an excavation and plunges a finger; I think it is a finger in my ass.

Not so bad I think but not fun. She is trying to get her cock in there and I can see her shadow humping away on the wall but its just not happening as she is not hard enough. 'You have a tight ass' she says. 'I am a virgin', I say, 'what do you expect'.

I don't like it anyway and once again begin to focus on the meat weapon I have to prepare. Lots of slow sucking and stroking, wanking and kissing later Am turns on to her stomach. 'Fuck me' she says and Cyn lies down to watch. 'Yai' (big), she laughs as she is not the one being put to the sword. 'You next' I tell her.

I impale Am and watch the tattoo on her back flinch in sympathy. Cyn begins to slap her roommate's arse as I fuck it. I like that very much indeed. This is the real deal; I am as high as a kite with a cock.

'Oh, that's it', Am moans through clenched teeth as she bites down on her tongue stud. She is a good little actor, give her due.

Cyn is wanking herself off as she watches which is fun.

Something is happening in my balls so I have to switch horses before its too late. Cyn has the biggest LB tits I have ever had the pleasure of fucking. Oil and water actually do mix against all popular opinion. If that water is spit. Her tits are fucking great.

I want Am on her back and it feels so good that the moment I enter her, I know it's game over. 'Deep', she shouts, 'Deeper', I wonder for a second if she is practicing her comparatives and wait for the superlative but too late comes that diversionary thought to stop me from unloading my wagon up her arse.

Oh Good god! I can recommend fucking to anyone who has never tried it; it feels great. We took photos then and Am practised her model walking up and down the loom to the Fashion TV theme tune she has on her blackcurrant phone. I am deadly serious, and so is she. Funny girl.

Eighteen

The Year of the Bunny

I am awoken by what sounds like cars crashing repeatedly into each other on my balcony, or is it outside the door? The sound is so loud I cannot tell. I remember I am alone.

Living opposite a Chinese temple seemed enchanting at the time I moved in. The drums and cymbals have woken the neighborhood and we all walk towards the sound. I follow, photograph and then find some food. Rice cakes, chicken, pork and jackfruit. Pretty good and 50baht.

After, I get a mystery phone call from 'Ice', 'Remember me?' 'We talk before online? I in Rama road, where you?'

'I wan see u'. 'I not pay, ok, I tell you before I not pay but if you want to meet for a coffee that's cool'. 'Ok', I come see you, I wan boyfriend know you more', DAWID, You pay for taxi?'

This feels like déjà-fuckin-vu. 'Ok, I pay for taxi', I say, generous to a fault. One hour later I wait outside in soi 6 and a taxi arrives.

She gets out looking like everything bad you ever wanted but were scared to ask for. So does a big, fat Thai man. 'Who the fuck is that', you ask politely. 'Oh 'she' my friend, come for way, he go eating when I with you'.

Eating was the last thing he looked like he needed. 'The food shops are that way', you indicate. 'She see loom then go waiting me' says Ice. You hold your tongue and get in the lift stopping at the reception area and sit down. They sit also. 'OK, this is as far as you go', you indicate the big fella. 'What you want, I told you I not pay'! The big fella's brow puckers. Here it comes, you think. 'He come only me ok' says the sexy one. 'Ok, but you both know, I NOT PAY OK, UNDERSTAND? NOT NEED SO YOU CAN GO NOW IF YOU WANT OK?'

'Understand', says sexy boots, 'Not want, want meet boyfriend, we can go loom and talk ok?'

In the loom you sit beside beauty and begin to take her in as she talks about nothing of any interest to you whatsoever.

Great tits, skin, fantastic tattoos, pretty face and mouth. 'So if we meet more I not bring she, ok, just for take care me', a reply is expected, 'Oh sure, I understand', she puts her hand on your leg and moves it about a bit.

She looks into your eyes with her big, blue ones and squeezes your stiffening cock. You are playing hard to get. 'Ok, you can do that if you want but I am still not paying you. 'On 'OK' she pulled down her pants to reveal a . . .well, a fucking great stiff cock, in fact the biggest stiffest cock you have seen unattached to your own body or on a ladyboy. 'Wow', you say, 'you're a big girl'! 'Dawid, you pay taxi ok,

200 baht to come and back na?' After a moment that passes as quickly as a hummingbird's forward stroke, you grab 400baht, 'No problem'. She is horny and after a bit of kissing and stroking she mounts you in the classic 69 position. Before her cock even gets in your mouth, she comes in a massive spurt like a small horse over your face and the bed. Impressive.

'I not fuck in long time' she says. Well let's do something about that, you think.

You are on top of her now, she is fucking sexy as hell and stinks like a fox. She tries to pull your cock into her arsehole but you stop her and get a condom (hard but do-able) You fuck her with ever increasing intensity. It's like shoving your face into a giant, sexed up ice cream. Soft, smooth mouthfuls of pleasure.

She is grimacing and whimpering a bit now and so you up the tempo and intensity because you are already reading 'red' on the temperature gauge. Not long now before she blows. This is really good. Too good and then it's over.

After you pull out there is blood on the condom and you thank your stars you wore it. After the bathroom two-step she calls someone and says, 'My friend ask if she can touch your big cock', 'Who, you ask, the bloke outside?', 'No, she Ladyboy'. Thinking another friend has arrived you get a bit excited but during clarification it transpires that apparently the big fat geezer waiting in reception is a lady' (boy). You are laughing now and she gets ready to go, opening the door for fatso to come in.

Sensing something not right you step up to the door. 'No you fucking don't', you block the door and push him back to a safe distance.

He stands there trying to grab your cock and making licking, sucking gestures with his mouth. You have never seen anything quite so horrible.

He keeps grabbing your cock as you are saying goodbye to beauty. 'Fuck off', you say and get her out of the room before whatever scam they are trying to pull can occur. Maybe he is just desperate for a shag.

He is fucking fat and ugly. Sadly, today he will sleep alone.

She calls from outside and in a stage whisper says, 'Dawid, next time I not bring she, ok'. 'NEXT TIME, ARE YOU JOKING?'

Sure, you say, next time!'

Nineteen

Oh-Satian, in her words.

My name Satian Say Satian, write Satiar.

I born close Buriram. Have sister live Pattaya have she boyfrien Australia. She not work bar now. Stay in loom.

Have two brother not same same fadder.

My fadder die long time. He work farmer drink, drink everyday. One day him not drink him not come home at middle of day and my mum she go look him

He sleeping with face in little water. Him dead. My mother go running to house she cry and me cry too. At night when all people go and him stay in box in loom downstair my sister see him eating at table. She have eight years and me ten.

I know I ladyboy from small because I like boy. I like girl too but like boy more. I like my friend. Him fuck me first time 12 year old. It hurt.

I finish school 12 year old and go Korat be monk. Dawid teasing me say I like be monk and be sexy little monk and fucking other monk. I say, 'Nooo, I no do, cannot say'. Him laughing for this.

When I finish monk I come Bangkok work in logo factory. Have short hair but wear little bit make-up to working.

I like Farang man always from small. I think I can meet boyfriend Farang in Pattaya so I go when 17 year old.

Before I go Pattaya I have my hair long and I go home to Buriram same same a lady and it ok. Make new name; 'Oh'. I choose because it sexy name.

I go work bar and I sure first man take me be my boyfriend. Him name Patrick, I remember. He not take me again. Not be my boyfriend. I not understand. Many men take me but not be my boyfriend.

I work many bar long time but not have many customer. I shy little bit and if customer like me can come talk with me but I not go only if they want.

I like make customer happy, then I happy. I stay Didi bar long time I like but not have many customer.

Have boyfriend Angritt him name Ralph. He go Englan, come back see me for two years. One day he say, 'You can go back to bar if you want, no problem, you want go?' I think him want me go so I say, 'Ok'. But I not want go. Not know why he throw me away.

Now I think he test me, see if I want go bar, but I not want. I not think too much now.

Dawid come Didi bar last year and I see him he looking at me but lady of bar sit with him. He not look at her, only me and Mama San say to lady she go. He say, 'You want have drink with me'?

He ask me, 'You lady or ladyboy'? Him not know sure. Look at my troat say, 'Good, Ladyboy'!

Him take me from bar. I like he. Him stay Sabai Empress hotel and he want go to eating after we make love. He pay me and I think he want me go because he pay me. I go back bar but want stay with him. He tell me yesterday he want me stay too but I not know.

Him go Vietnam call me every day on phone. Missing him.

He come Pattaya and I stay with him one time in Skytop hotel. Him come bar with me later walking. We eating and him talk with my friends, I think he like she, he say No. I stay with him then.

Next time him come Pattaya we stay same same place and have ghost in loom. We see and make loud bang, bang on wardrobe. Dawid phone alarm go off many times but phone turn off not on? How can, only spirit because hotel have not spirit house. We both scarey.

Him tell me have grlfriend in Bangkok but finished with she. I like he too much and he take me party in Nong Bar meeting many Ladyboy and Farang.

I go to Bangkok and happy but we in loom and she come knock, knock on door. He go talk with she and I think he lie me. Have girlfriend. He tell me go back Pattaya.

I come back now and we together for one week. I like he same same and he like me. He old little bit but ok.

We meet him friends Guess Bar my friend from Pattaya working and talk with many Ladyboy. Them say me, 'not scared off big cock?' because I small Ladyboy. I say. 'No'. Him laughing but only look me.

I go Pattaya today look for business and come back soon. Leave clothes in him loom. He say he not throw away.

She has been in Buriram with her mother whose mind is disappearing fast She says little but it is always telling 'My mum want my blood, she is too thin' 'My mum speak crazy'

She is so brown you do not recognise her when she steps from the taxi. She looks every inch a farmer's daughter and straight from the farm. The pig nose seller says, 'Farang not like brown lady'. How does he know?

You knew that if she did not come and stay with you would fall back into the same old pattern with Farida.

Her calling and your love-struck and futile resistance crumbling before watching her go to work later unless you were 'taking care of her financially'.

You think she is truly and stupendously unaware that although she is a gorgeous ladyboy, there are many more equally or more attractive out there many of whom do not expect to be paid or kept women who do nothing all day while you work! She is a soulless bitch but it's taken you awhile to be strong enough to admit.

Now you are stronger.

Minutes after Satian walks upstairs on shiny brown legs you are kissing, touching, fucking.

'I want you hurt me', she said last time you met. Now she is regretting such a bold statement.

Your mother used to say, 'Be careful what you wish for, it may come true'. 'Slowly, slowly, she says, 'I not do for long time'.

She is a superstar of sex. She loves doing it, laughing about it, trying it and gives the best blowjob you ever, EVER had.

She has a big cock and is always hard. 'Would you like to fuck me every time we have sex?', you ask. "Yes, she laughs, embarrassed'!

Bangkok, you have a lot to answer for. You are a lucky man. So why are you so fucked up on Farida?

This girl has her beat hands down in terms of sheer sexiness, generosity and actions speaking louder than words.

Every day she stays you like her more and more and you tell her so.

She is going back to Pattaya, you tell her you know she will go back to the bar; it's where her friends are.

You tell her you will not tell her not to go with customers, it's her life.

You know that the excitement and adoration LB's get from customers is sometimes too much too resist and imagine yourself a 25yr old man facing the prospect of being paid for sex.

The downside is that most customers are old, fat and ugly.

But that's what kamagra's for right. Still, easy money and you get to come a couple of times a night at least.

You know what you would say to that, 'Bring it on!' Maybe she will go back to the bar, maybe she will go with a customer or two? She asks you to promise you will not fuck any other Ladyboys; 'Wait for me'?? You have no idea what you will do that very night never mind a weeks time!

She is going back to Pattaya to research some potential business. If she can handle it, she could be your girl.

If not; well, the bargirl/LB mentality stops so many of them from getting the little clothes shop/ beauty shop they all say they want.

If it were as true as they all say it is, 'I work short time only, save money for business', then every dress shop in Bangkok would be owned by a ladyboy ex-prostitute wouldn't it?

Like always, you expect too much. In the words of the song,

I want a girl with a mind like a diamond I want a girl who knows what's best I want a girl with shoes that cut And eyes that burn like cigarettes. With fingernails that shine like justice And a voice that is dark like tinted glass.

This can only be a Ladyboy, it's the Ladyboy song right?

You try to capture part of Oh's story on video but she is too video camera shy bless her. She makes you laugh almost every time she speaks. She is beautiful inside and out. She is a great girl and maybe, just maybe all mine?

Twenty

Valentines Day Massacre

Today I put things to rest. Said goodbye to my heart and closed a chapter of my life. I met my beloved Farida and we walked like gods amongst the mortals.

A ladyboy and her consort.

But gods can fall. Mark this day.

Letting go of her has been like dying. I have needed time to say goodbye to the world we built.

My resolve has crumbled under her desire to 'have it all'; a boyfriend and customer's money.

She wanted a rose, I bought her one . . .she did not know it was to say goodbye.

My attempts to escape from this toxic, beautiful relationship have been made easier by my loving friendship with Oh.

Mark the day.

Farida wanted to go out tonight, Valentine's Day. I told her to go to work. Wear her rose and a red dress (for blood)

Oh is back in Pattaya for a few days to see her friends.

'I only go bar for drink, talking not go with customers, I not want you go with other Ladyboy.

Promise me you won't do', she said.

I knew this was too good to be true. Mark the day.

A new sim card and a Scots accent and 'John' made the fateful call.

John-'Hello, is that Oh? I saw you afore Christmas and you gave me a number.

Well I am back in Pattaya now and want to meet you'. Oh-'you want meet me, what your name?' John-'John'. Oh-'Where are you'?

John-'I am at the Baywalk Residence, Beach road, I not want to come to the bar, when can you come to my hotel?'

Mark the day.

Oh-'Send me SMS where you are, I come now' John-'Ok, call me when you are outside and i will come down and get you'.

And just like that, it was done.

15 minutes pass while I studied my deceit, and prepared for what is to come, before the phone call.

Oh-'I outside now, you come for me?'

'Ok, I come down now . . . oh, wait, there is someone here who wants to speak with you'.

John left for Glasgow.

Hello Oh, I said. Do you recognise my voice? 'Yes. Dawid' Her voice already breaking, crying.

I trusted you Oh, you asked me not to go with other Ladyboys while you were away for 4 days.

You told me you did not want to go with customers.

We planned a business together. You lied to me. You know how much I liked you. 'I only come to see' 'No'. 'Your friend he trick me come here'. 'No friend Oh, only me', nothing more to say. I see you no more, I cannot trust you'. In a voice from the end of all hope I said,'Goodbye Satian'.

Mark the day.

Mark the day that the red rose of St. Valentine closed. Mark the day that all love closed Mark the day that I finally grew up. Mark the day. No more tears Mark the day. Honey arrives from outside of the city at 12am. I have two hours to grow a new heart, or not? Mark the day

Twenty One

The next day we go to Chatuchak; 'buy plants Khun Dawid', Farida jokes. Her plants always die. She does not water them. She persuades me toward the fish market area. She likes goldfish.

We spent two sweaty hours buying 24 various fish and a tank. On the way back to the market she slaps me, 'Why you not stop me spent 500baht on fishes!' I tell her that it is the equivalent of a blow- job she need not have given. She is upset to have spent the money and I tell her I know what she is thinking. She will not be happy until she recoups the loss tonight at Nana. One customer = 1000baht minimum and when she has that she will feel 'sabai jai'. 500baht to the good and fish to boot.

I tell her that when she watches her fish she can think of me.

Every tiny golden fish, a tear.

When we get home, I help fill the tank and walk to my apartment. She tells me we have not made love for a long time, she wants to come tonight. I know it is just a pretty lie.

Half an hour passes and she calls me, 'I watch fish and I miss you Dawid'. I know she will not come.

From the markets to the temples, to the jails and the bars across this city the same story is being told many times in many different ways. From the cradle to the grave it has ever been so. Sweet lies told to a lover, good intentioned, sweet, sweet lies. But lies all the same.

In the 7/11 the bottles of 100 Pipers whisky are shouting, 'Wake Up, don't you remember the last time? She took a customer to her room, to your place, Wake up you sick fool. He bought us in here, she was on his arm, his girlfriend for the afternoon, We watched as he took off her clothes, as he squeezed her brown nipples, as she sucked his cock. We watched his nameless face contort as he came inside her, your woman. Wake from your sleep, dreamer, sweet as it is you must wake up or this will end down some midnight deep soi with one death or two.

As you step outside the soi is ablaze with your funeral pyre, a fiery death that is happening somewhere between truth and fantasy. You shed another layer of skin. Wounded but still alive.

She cannot come, she slept too long and you did not call her. She goes to work. You arrange a date, a knockout drop, a cure.

Soi 5 is overrun with drug dealers, you begin to imagine murders dark and violent. A beautiful girl sits on the hood of a taxi, drinking from a bottle. You wait for Nan to arrive.

Farida calls, 'want to go for drinking, come for me. I wait for you'. No, No, No, LEAVE ME ALONE!' You scream into the tiny phone in your swelling fist. The girl climbs down off the taxi.

Beauty is late arriving and you walk to Nana to take one last stab at romance. Again. You see her face on every girl you pass. Every window holds her ghost. Every farang is her next customer. They are mocking you, mocking your whole fucking life. Something bad begins to happen.

You see her walking up Soi 3 from a short time room. One half-hour has passed since she called you. You cannot breath or speak. Her face is so beautiful, so gentle, so distant. The storm breaks inside you. You limp away on your stunted spirit. She stands in the middle of the soi calling after you. Did you see her?

You send Beauty home. You are full with something so putrid, so rotten, that you know you will vomit sometime soon. Beauty is an innocent bystander. Even you have some scruples. You catch sight of yourself in the mirror, look away quickly. You cannot meet your own eyes.

2AM, She walks along Sukhumvit, she knows where you will be. Her radar never fails. Between soi 5 and 7, the final chapter in tonight's Bangkok story is about to be written.

Twenty Two

I usually sit on Sukhumvit late at night or in the early hours. I am 65 years old but I still like to stay up late, sleep late. I sit outside so I can smoke my pipe, watch the passers by.

She arrived at about 2am; a beautiful prostitute . . . she went straight to his table. I had been watching him wait for something . . . for her. A typical sexpat, shaved head, big, muscled, ignorant. I have seen so many of them in my years here. But now I had to think again; she was a kathoey. Mmmmn?

He had smoked three cigarettes in the short time I had watched him. I like watching. He stood up when she arrived, almost as if he was standing to attention; rigid, waiting for something.

She sat and spoke to him. They were lovers, that was clear. I smiled, he smiled, spoke, touched her arm and in a gesture that only Thai people can do; she touched his forehead with the palm of a long fingered hand and laughed. Called him, 'Khun Dawid'. Her gesture was commonplace between them . . . but tonight was different somehow.

Something was wrong.

I am a keen observer of people and I began feeling slightly unsettled. He ordered food, drink, they talked. I went back to my paper and the girls at the front of the massage place went back to their chatter.

I looked back at them and he seemed to swell without moving at all. He said something like, 'Take your long face back to Nana then, go on, just fuck off'.

She said, 'Dawid stop'.

He grabbed a bottle of beer and threw it in her face covering her in beer and stood up, throwing the table over as he did. Every face turned toward the couple. Froze. He was pouring more beer over her. I was frightened. I kept still, hoped he didn't look at me. He was bellowing and throwing chairs around now like a stupid, brutish bull.

English. Typical English behaviour. The kathoey was covered in beer now but strangely calm. She just kept saying, 'Dawid, stop, Dawid, stop, stop'. He didn't stop, I could see he was out of control. The massage girls were screaming now and the food shop people had become animated but no one went near him. Plates, food, glass and furniture were all over the soi. A crowd who could not get past the mess gathered at the edge of the horrible display. What an ignorant yob he was. He couldn't even make any sense only shouting, 'Fuck you', you cunt', at the top of his lungs in every direction. He was red and ugly. She was wet, cold, mostly silent. He pushed her, pushed her, no-one stopped him. I am old.

He began to walk away, thank God, but the food shop woman shouted after him for her money; '380 BAHT!' 'What, he said! 'Fuck off', and threw two hundred baht notes at her. 'Keep away from me' he shouted at the kathoey and walked away into the traffic.

The massage girls gathered around the kathoey now, gave her tissue. She did not smile or speak. A girl wiped her face, breast, arms clean. She walked after him like a zombie. Good luck to her. The crowd watched her go, 'Farangs!' said the food shop owner. 'Kathoeys!' said a massage girl.

Twenty Three

I had a reckoning in Bangkok late last night. Travis rode the silver bullet over the Chonburi state line to be where the action was. Across the city Beauty shares a cab with J to the hangout on 22. The made men sit drinking warm beer in the evenings soft heat The New Yorker pulls into town figures it all out from the signs in the book of Leviticus. He carries it for the benefit of the strangers that sojourn in this holy land. Keeping the laws of the jungle at bay is a life's work. So midnight's men are met at their rendezvous for the night beneath that giant Emporium sign that brings so much joy if not to us then to the hearts of our Ladyboys. They are ours, after all is said and done. There's a carnival every night out on Sukhumvit and a dance that is measured in steps between the hungry and the hunted as they face off against each other. Nobody knows which is which.

But nocturnal contracts are made and they disappear together only to reappear alone, empty. The streets are alive with secret debts overdue, assignations, partings. Promises made, 'never again' and a police siren rips apart the strange sanctity of the Nana Jungle. It's Big Buddha Night. Again.

In the Nana parking lot the mai tam mesha sport the latest 'Paris' fashion. Those fresh from Isaan just sport flesh. Fashion TV plays in the corner bar. The girls down here are like ghosts; insubstantial, transparent, just a look and a whisper, and they're gone. Just a whiff of truth or daylight, they disappear. A saxophone is playing a familiar tune. But beneath the transport arteries of the city two hearts beat, beat, beat. I am putting paid to a dream. My ancestors have lived it many times before. I have run too much, to far from their words. Running has bought me here. Running, I have lost my home but still I keep on running and now I am crawling, crawling like a black spider . . . and across the city in a bedroom locked against the night the Gun Girl has turned off the Love Removal Machine as I turn mine on.

Connected, rejected, resurrected. The Ghost box whirrs in the night air, the stars look down. The police stand by. Do nothing. 'Will you catch me if I fall?' A drunk is repeating over and over as he walks bewildered up Soi 4. He has been here too long, not long enough. The Tiny Godfather sweats his face free of bread he has not earned, blesses me, washes his hands again. Baptised by the New Yorker, I know I ain't got long. The clock is ticking now, tick, tock, tick, tock goes the taxi meter before it arrives.

Tick, tock go the voices of Beauty and J.

Tick, tock goes the chamber of Gungirl's revolver as she loads her silver bullet.

Tick, tock, tick goes my heart on it's final gentle passage.

Beauty arrives, awkward, thinking . . . too much. We go to make peace; me, J and Beauty. All white, all long gone. All looking for some kind of redemption in the flowers and the long walk three times around the temple.

Beauty is cracked. Lost. Asks me for directions over and over. Watches me for a sign. None comes. I have forgotten my way too. Across the city Gun Girl looks in the mirror, moves her hands just so . . . . . At the Wongwain Yai roadside Beauty feeds green shoots to the clay oven moves her hands just so. . I turn off the Love Removal machine too late. Gun Girl points the revolver at the mirror, loads the chamber, tick, tock goes the trigger, tick, tock goes silver bullet. Tick, tock goes the bullet as she fires into the dark mirror, and on a balcony across the burning city a bullet that has grown old in it's waiting rips through the night. Shooting me down. The shot echoes down every soi, blows back the curtains of every house that hides the Molotov cocktails, nail bombs, land mines, bullets, tear gas, and rocks that missed.

Her Love does not miss.

No one watches when the ambulance pulls away or as the Gun Girl turns out the bedroom light.

Outside The New Yorker shakes his head, knew what was coming too soon. An honest stand'l hurt you in this city of angels; leave you scarred, dangerous.

In the morning Travis and the New Yorker walk among the lovers through the fallen cherry blossoms outside Benjasiri Park.

Travis: Wabi, feckin what? New Yorker: Sayonara Sakura. You had to fall.

Twenty Four

Cherry: 'I love you Dawid'. 4 days in to our 'relationship'.
'No, you fuckin don't, you don't know me never mind love me!
'Don't say like dat darleeng'
'Stop calling me darleeng, you can't say it properly, your not French,

your from Laos! It just sounds silly, and you've got bad breath, by the way'.

It's a sex roles thing.

I am sick at home and she says she will come to 'take care of me'. What she means is that she will come over dressed like the biggest, sexiest big- breasted ladyboy slut imaginable and insist she fuck me better. She has a massive organ and frankly, it does nothing for me!!! I am Top, she's a Top!

I agreed to it because she is fucking gorgeous and I made a rule, remember. 'Never say No to a new experience!

There is some latent pleasure there in watching her urgent expression change and her eyes roll back in her head when she comes and flops down on top off me like a spent hosepipe

There is some latent pleasure in holding and stroking her smooth skinned back and arse while she is plunging in and out of me! Fucking hell, what have I become!!!

A Ladyboy's bitch is what!!!! No, No, No, this cannot happen!

It's an intellectual and spiritual angst thing.

What is happening inside my head is a re assessment of my status as the plug as opposed to the socket. Am I a little bit less masculine now? Will it come back if I STOP now or is my Mojo gone for good? Has it slunk away in disgust like a rat leaving a sinking ship?

It's a compatibility thing!

She is a Scorpio, I am a Scorpio . . . get the picture? Too much of everything together in the same room, bed . . . . .a recipe for something too bad to eat.

It's a jealousy thing 'Please can you do one thing for me dahleeng?' Can you delete every picture of another ladyboy from your Facebook account (the one she knows about) I don't want my friends to see my boyfriend and then see he has many ladyboy girlfriends in his loom, I can see the bed, the wall, the window oooohhh, too many, it hurt my heart to see', please, I can delete for you.

'OK' (I have all the pictures so don't give a fuck) and I am too lazy to do it myself, have at it Cherry. She was still doing it an hour later! It's a convenient thing, is what it is . . .

or in the words of the New Yorker on hearing what I am about to share with you all 'How fucking convenient is that, man?'

I knew, for all the above reasons that despite her being a sensational, if jealous, girl, that this relationship does not have legs!

Because . . . and here it comes. .

It's a Farida thing. That crazy, uncompromising little girl just won't quit.

Cannot forget her, no matter what I do, who I fuck, what she does. She is the one and only. How fucked up is that? She is pretty, sure but I can resist that. She is a ruthless bitch whose every move is about making money from customers.

But, she fucking loves me. What she does with me is not motivated by money How do I know? Because I have none! Not a fucking cent. I met her tonight after a week of poison SMS's to each other . . .a tornado meeting a tidal wave, terrible, heartbreaking dreadful words . . . all because we love each other and cannot walk away clean . . . not without losing a part of ourselves . . . a lung, a liver, an arm, a heart . . . that kind of loss won't grow back. I know. I lost an eye to a girl in England ten years ago.

We declared our love for each other again and I smiled for the first time in 3 weeks. I saw her smile too, which was even better, better than a million stars in any sky you care to name. We love each other and I will have to deal with the nights like tonight when she is at Nana; how much do I loathe that place now. So, I am sitting by my computer tonight with a happy heart and the phone rings - - -

Hi, I saw you Thai friendly . . .

What your name baby?

Neung (or something like that???)

Oh, did i send you a message?

Yes, I want meet wid u, can?

Wait a minute (checking my outgoing messages) I didn't send you a message, don't recognise your name?

Oh . . .

How did you get my number? (Sterner tone adopted here) Hang up tone.

Half a minute later Hello?

I see you before, I dancer at Bayonne. You got girlfriend now? Mmmn (smelling and recognising the voice of a Laotian rat) Yes Ok bye I sent an SMS.

Tell your friend cherry. No call me more. Bye cherry!

Half a minute Cherry calls Hi Dahleeng I know it was you, on the phone Sorry, wat u mean dahleeng? Pretending to ask me on a date. I KNOW IT WAS YOU CHERRY!

Haaa (nervous laughter, how easy they crack under a little pressure) I call on my friend phone, only want to know you my boyfriend . . . for sure, and you say YES! I happy now.

Ask me again. What dahleeng? Ask me again if I have a girlfriend

Oh, you have girlfriend?

NO. Bye. Click.

'Just enough brains to think up a lie or a trick but never enough brains to pull it off' says the New Yorker later.

And of course, 'How fucking convenient is that?' They cannot outfox the fox says I!

Twenty Five

She is back in my bed again.

Back in my heart again.

As we exit the MRT at Huay Kwang the sky is heavy.

'It rain', she says.

'Storm come', I say.

I ask her why she wants to pray.

'I think you know Dawid'.

I have no idea.

She holds my hand as I almost trip over the shoes piled at the entrance.

The heavy smoke of incense hangs in the air. Can you smell it?

Sweat is pouring from my head. It is difficult to see.

A garland of yellow flowers and a bunch of joss sticks are thrust toward

me. She looks at me quizzically as if I should know what to do.

She takes my hand again, leads me to a space on the floor.

I kneel beside her. I am the only farang in the shrine. 'You must have a wish in your heart, koh jai mai, understand?' she says.

'Yes', I say numb with something . . . . . spiritual? Something theatrical, something otherworldly?

I feel her hair against my naked arm. A shock runs through my body and a wave of happiness washes through my stupid, senseless, hopeful heart.

She is praying and holding the burning joss sticks in her palms. I, like a child, copy my teacher. I pray and in praying, I mean everything I say. Ganesh, remove from my heart the bloated pride, the bitterness, the longing, the envy, the brutality, the violence, the jealousy, the desire to be adored that is stopping me from loving this woman by my side no matter what she does for a living.

Stopping me from finding simple happiness and the love I have searched for all my life . . .and failed to find or rejected so many times. Ganesh, let someone love me . . . a lonely man, in this strange and beautifully fucked up country . . .

Ganesh, let her love me, let her understand that love is not money, not something you can buy. Let her see my heart and understand that I am only a man. I too can break.

We stand and make our offerings of flowers, water, milk and incense. The sweat running down my face covers the tears. She pretends she does not see. We shake wooden vases filled with numbered sticks until one falls out.

Her number is 13, mine 3. She rips a sheet of Thai script for each number from a pad hanging on the wall. We leave. I buy her a fabric rose from the street, it may outlive the Valentine rose. She smiles, hugs me. I am transported. A foolish balloon buoyed up on her affection.

We sit at a strange terrace bar in Ratchada and listen to an acoustic duo sing and play sad Thai pop songs, drink Singha and eat coconut fish. She reads the Thai script. It is written in 'old' Thai and difficult for her to translate.

She says I have a 'hot' heart and have many problems as it makes me 'sick inside'; unhappy. Money is hard for you to find, she looks at me meaningfully.

She tells me that she prayed for us. She made a vow to Ganesh, 'If we can be married, I will make an offering of fruit'.

I begin to tell her my wish, 'I know what you wish for Dawid'.

My perception of what is real and what is not is not is fracturing, unpeeling the longer I am in this country.

She reads her script, 'I will always find money. That will never be a problem for me. But I am like a tree that bears no fruit and in the hot, dry season has no water'. She begins to cry as she reads this part.

Tears run down her face and she quickly wipes them away. We look at each other and in that look our future is writ. This moment will never pass. When we lay dying, this moment will stand as a monument to what could have been but never was.

I pull her close and whisper in her ear, 'I will be your water'. She lays her head on my shoulder in a gesture that is so much more than words. If she could make me understand that her heart is mine and that her body is just meat we could be happy. But I am farang. No matter how I try, I cannot share any part of her. That night we sleep together, the touch of her hair, her skin, her breathing, so precious to me and so easily forgotten by any other man.

I will never recover from this night, from this girl. There is not enough life left in me, not enough time left for me to forget her. I am utterly lost. Ganesh; Help me please.

Twenty Six

Alive again. You smell the air and begin to sense your surroundings. A feckless breeze lifts the solitary food wrapper from the waste ground on Sukhumvit road and blows it fast against the side of the ambulance parked in the entrance to the dead end soi under the giant neon crucifix. Bangkok; it is what it is. Don't try to understand it, just feel it, breathe it. 'Reese', is the most visible of the words on the wrapper.

Inside the ambulance you gasp and sit up like a drowned man risen from the darkness of a deep lake. Resurrection Joe. Your clothes are still smoking from the ghost bullet that shot you down. The orderlies move away from the ambulance, dropping their cigarettes as you step from the rear doors and smell the breeze. Which way is the wind blowing? What is your name today weightless one?

You walk a step or two; try your luck on the street. Buddhism; gotta love it. The Dutchman sits with someone else's beauty.

She is on the clock and he's punching way above his class if not his weight but the Landmark is a landmark he wants to be seen enjoying. The beauty is being paid to speak Engleesh and listen to his broken life story.

You stalk the S street markets keeping a low glow in the dim neon darkness. The soi 3 faces turn to you. They recognise the 'Walking Tall' tattoo and the 'Red Rooster'. The faces mouth incalculable curses to ward off the voodoo in your eye.

You go to her.

Much later after everything that was done and said has been spewed up like a cow's innards and lays spread across the table that stands between you, you sleep, together, again.

You wake, watch her face; Mona Lisa's little sister. You see no guilt, no pain, no regrets. She is a creature of the wind. She is a Djinn, a child of the smoke. As the gun still smokes she dreams of big money jobs, no boom boom, quick and coming clean for a getaway back to you? You stopped dreaming six months ago the first time you put your hands around her throat when you were fucking her. That was dream enough. Nowadays your skin burns when she comes near, burns hotter when she is not there by your side. The more she smokes, the more you burn, like CS gas, she burns you.

In Khlong San a migration is happening. A demographic ripple of

Ladyboys. A killer in a red dress collides with you as she L's around the Lotus chicken stand. Her eyes flick to your face and away. You shouldn't be here, not now. She does not turn on her red light until the Sky train tannoy sings, 'Nana'.

Neung, Noy, Oil and Ploy have come to live on soi 6 with Sod, Gate, Aye and Aui. It's getting crowded, soon there will be more number 3's here than at the plaza mouth.

The mosquitoes bite me and my skin burns with sweat. It's midnight in Silom, Bangkok and I am waiting for my sweetheart. She is upstairs in Lumpini Tower fucking a customer for 3000 baht. She is longer than the usual 45 minutes. 'He cannot come', she says, 'hard work, use 5 condoms, boom- boom, rest, wanking him, boom-boom, wanking, ayyyy!

I come and I think I finish and him cannot come, tammi? He a young guy!

I watched him as he met her in the lobby earlier. I stood back in the darkness assessing him and my potential passage through security and up inner doorway. Young, big, but lacking in social skills and a little awkward. 'He a teacher, him scared security see I am a ladyboy. He put me in elevator in dark I come down from him apartment. I scared but can turn light on when I inside'.

While I wait, I smoke too much.

We ride home together in a cab holding hands and shower together like children covering each other in soap, laughing, happy, relieved.

As we fall asleep I wonder what this relationship is about and how it works. She is part lover, part daughter, part mother and part son to me and underneath the tensions, jealousies, her job and our disagreements is love, understanding, compassion and companionship holding us together. Neither of us has found this before and perhaps we never will again. That's why I whisper to her, 'we cannot lose each other, we have to hold on'. She says, 'Hug me'. How can this be real? This love between me and an Asian ladyboy named Num Sod (Fresh Milk.) Life is closer to the edge here in Bangkok. You are watching your footing, waiting for the slip or blessed break. That day when she rests from the disunity and disharmony, from everything that is not you and she.

One day you will face the music, pay the piper, come to a sticky end. But not today. Today you will walk talk, again.

Twenty Seven

Drinking Saeng Som opens up all kinds of doors so I won't dress what follows in logical clothes, just let it come . . . I am in a bad way. I just saw a ghost on the roof of a new building opposite mine in Khlong San . . . where do all the old Ladyboys go?

Farida is preparing for work:

Hi this is Malcom from Gay Romeo, how are you?

Can we meet?

Tonight? How much you can pay me?

Ok, well, 1500baht just for sex, but I want much more than that!

How much you can pay?

Ok I can pay you 2500baht for drinks and dinner and then if you want to have sex we can talk about it, ok?

Where you want take me?

Well, I want to take you in the ass LOL, seriously, I know a nice restaurant I will take you.

You can dress casual jeans is ok or a dress

I wear dress, ok?

Ok well don't look too elegant or all the men in the restaurant will want you, save it for your wedding dress when we get married! LOL Can you make it 7.30?

See you at the Tawanna Hotel, Silom, Hugs, Malcom xxxxx

This is the SMS conversation she had with a customer from Gay Romeo, a dating site.

Sorry if you are Malcom or if you are angered or insulted by the content herein. I tell it like it is.

She has gone to meet him. It is 7.57 on the 20th April, year of our lord 2011.

The news report talks about the Christian Crusade against the unholy Muslim religion. Nothing has changed much, now we are making films about killing Arabs as well as doing it with a vengeance.

Jealousy and fucking are old fashioned phenomena.

I have done lots of the latter and so must suffer lots of the former?

That's Buddhism right? Karma?

I have spent three balmy weeks with my Ladyboy.

I feel loathe to use the word lover, partner, darling, best friend, love of my fucking life although she is all of them, not sure why?

The SMS convo happened on the way home from Palookaville (Pattaya).

Songkran in that city mocked our plans of getting to Jomtien, and after spending a truly beautiful Songkran festival in Surin and Silom, I did not need to see farangs brandishing water pistols. The real thing happened last week. You don't even know what the festival is about! In Surin we were the toast of the town. I was a kind of totem, a good luck charm to be blessed and give blessings in return. I was moved, touched by Thai men and women alike . . . loved in a bleary alcoholic kind of way. It was like growing up in the 70's. Beautiful, man.

Pattaya was something else. Something ugly, competitive.

I am ok! I told her after helping her with her English replies to Malcom. I know what u do.

She tells me everything, shows me everything . . . there is no sophistry between us. She is a businesswoman.

I help her talk to customers because I want her to be safe and make the money I cannot give her to survive. Sounds easy right?

I am doing fine, right?

Wrong.

Loving her too much is my destiny, loving me too much is her . . . destiny?

She's 24. Prostitute for eighteen months.

Right now she is talking to him, eating dinner in a place I cannot afford. Later he will take off her dress, she will smile . . . he will kiss her, Oh God help me because even that is too much to bear.

He will fuck her in the ass for another 1000baht.

SMS-Don't cry my moo yai, I not die, I come home to you tonight xxxxx

She does, every night, sometimes smelling like a used condom.

Writing that hurt.

SMS-I go tonight and I no have to go to Nana can be with you.

She has not been to Nana for 3 weeks. Kikiat, she says, but really because she does not want. She wants to be with me.

No alter ego can save me from what I feel now.

I love her too, too much but I am pinned to the wall of my apartment by a steel pole through my heart.

I can't move, think, breath. Only feel, like a paper lantern twisting in a flame.

I have been helping her find customers who can pay more than the 1000baht she demands at Nana.

Higher paying customers, less sex, more safety? Whenever I help her I get sick.

I know its better she has less but something is aching to spew itself out of my mouth across every table we sit at and eat.

She sees me cry, every time she goes to work, she worries, holds my hand, tells me she loves me, it is alright, not for long now, you find better job, we have business together.

When I say, 'Enough', I cannot take it any more . . . she comes to my room, sits on my chest and makes me listen to her Thai logic, which is no logic at all. She just talks and kisses me.

Can I stand by her? I am no saint.

This is not a piece of writing mellowed by a little time friends, this is happening NOW. It's 8.35 and RIGHT NOW SHE IS WITH MALCOM.

HELP ME. Is Love enough? He is fucking my woman, probably right now.

I have no fears about sex but I am a nightmare with no money. No, she won't leave me for another. She loves me with every bit of her. But she gives every bit of herself to customers, at least her beautiful body. I call the New Yorker and thank him for listening to my bullshit and pain. I nearly fucking cried when he said, 'It's OK Man'. He is a gentleman and I just needed a friendly voice that understood.

Twenty Eight

I wait by the river for my boat to work. No matter how exotic the paradise a day at work is like any other. The river stinks.

Every time I go to the toilet in Bankapi Mall, which is often, just to relieve the boredom, it is full of Femboys fussing with their hair and lipstick in the mirrors. They are waiting for the day they can become Ladyboys or escape to Pattaya and meet a Farang whom they think will have a more open attitude to sexuality, to gender than their parents, than Thai people in general. They may wait a considerable time for their Mr. Right. They may experience the company of many Mr. Rights along the way. So it goes.

Last night we found a new food shop to eat in on our soi. A young Thai girl works at fetching and carrying. She has recently come from Isaan to help her uncle and aunt run the shop. She watches us as if she is watching a glamorous TV soap, with her mouth open. She is tall and awkward with her teenage self. We are taller, assured and romantic as we smile, kiss and hold hands openly. She does not see the tears I cry when we leave and Farida goes to work but she helps to make the place somewhere we will visit often.

Farida does not spend so much time at Nana now, Craigslist is becoming a lucrative and much saner modus operandi so we spend many beautiful evenings together doing precisely nothing.

The dumb questions sent by email from craigslist are at once a source of amusement, alarm and a little sadness; 'How big is your cock, can you come, can you come to Tim-buk-Too, I pay for taxi and tip you 500 baht, can you send me more pictures off your cock'. The questions are usually accompanied by pictures of the customers cock spattered with semen as if this will encourage her to fuck them for free. I guess some people are just unreafuckinglistic or deluded?

In between answering the dumb questions and meeting the genuine customers we watch an animated cartoon from Farida's teenage past called Sailor Moon. It's the ladyboy development blueprint.

A gang of sexy Japanese supergirls do battle with evil often in the form of well-endowed female harpies. It's easy to see how she loved this cartoon. When they fight the super-girls transform and call on the power of make-up to help their endeavours. A compact and a lipstick appear on the screen and the girls are made even more super, stronger, faster and more awesome in every way. They become invincible and gain special powers depending on the make-up. It is a ladyboy fantasy complete.

Farida watches eagerly, laughing girlishly and adopting the poses of her special hero, Sailor Mars, a dark haired beauty. I smile and enjoy participating in such a beautiful memory. I love her trust in me. I love her more every day.

I travel most days by sky-train and study the Thais I see. I am trying to learn a new language, lexicon of life and love in this fair country. 08.15 and a Thai girl stands apart from the usual sleepy commuters. They look at her, frown, look away feeling justified in their disapproval. She is wearing last night's cocktail dress. Everyone here wears a uniform even the lowliest civil servant but hers isolates her outside of Nana, Patpong.

She is returning from a customer's apartment or hotel. She holds my gaze, smiles. She looks tired. I ask her, 'Khun baynay'? 'Where do you go?'

She sits by me as we sit and tells me a piece of her life. Two months (it's always two months or so) she came from Isaan to work in a bar. She had been in my building with a farang I don't know. Maybe it was the crazy professor or the academic or the hippy?

It wasn't Ray. I am pleased. He is an asshole. He spoke to me only once when he was so drunk a taxi driver begged me to help remove him from the cab. He threatened me and everyone around him as I helped him to his room. He avoided my gaze from then on but Farida told me he was at Nana soliciting Ladyboys who refused his generosity and beer bellied proposals of 1000baht to go back with him to Khlong San for the night. They know better than to spend their time. They laughed and called to each other across the plaza mouth, 'Anyone want to go for 1000baht to Khlong San with this asshole, he's very generous! He looks sulkily at Farida and I when we see him walking on our soi. He is a man who does not like ladyboys. Not openly. He has lots of company in Bangkok.

Marie says goodbye to me at Siam and then pushes me in the back as I wait for my train to Chid-lom. She doesn't know her way around yet but gets off the train at Asoke. She's just another child at war with herself and so is Ray. If there is a god up there it's time he shone some light down here amongst the loveless.

On my way home I sit across from a Thai boy and girl. They have the clothes on their backs and a cardboard box. First day from Isaan. He has a hard, tough stare and looks me straight in the eyes. I like him immediately. She leans against him in her dirty t-shirt and flip-flops, like a puppy. She looks sixteen but is probably fourteen. They look like runaways from a family that would not allow them to be together. He is probably a problem child. Tattooed across the left hand side of his face are the words, 'Stop Love', in bold, undeniable print. He relaxes a little after I smile at them. I have fallen in love with the idea of them. She does not seem to notice the tattoo as she leans against his shoulder and tilts her chin up to kiss his cheek. He, forgetting himself, squeezes her hand tighter and smiles into her eyes. I am made happy. I wish them luck when I step off the train. She says 'Ka'. He smiles. Passing souls are perfect. They will never age in my memory, never die. Beauty lives on.

Twenty nine

I can't meet you today, I go to hospital, see doctor, make my breasts. I meet her 4 days later. She arrives 20 minutes late on high heels and just inside a tiny red mini-skirt. The doctor is to be commended. Her tits look great inside the little t-shirt she is wearing.

She is breathtakingly beautiful down to the un-split ends of her long black hair.

Later we sit in the 'Bug and Bee', a farang-orientated café cum restaurant in Silom. The 'we' of the moment are 'Beachlife',

He is an engaging and switched on Californian from the north of that state. He brings his date of the moment 'Chang –Mai'. Beachlife's dates don't tend to last too long; he is as the bee to the flower so this restaurant is apt. Shame about the food!

His girl's Thai nickname is 'Pinky', but between us we call her Chang-Mai because it sounds cooler. We are definitely sitting with the two most gorgeous 'girls' in the establishment and probably in Silom. We are a pair of lucky fuckers, quite literally.

We cannot buy alcohol but sneak glasses of red wine from the bottle we bought with us. The girls are both concerned. Thai people can be so law- abiding and conservative. We cannot drink because it is the night before voting in Thailand, the night before Taksin's sister and new leader of the Peau Thai party sweep to power. The red-shirt violence and radicalism has not put off enough voters to halt their victory. Taksin is back!

Focus, that's my beauty's name, is staring at me and so I stare back. The difference between our stares is that she is 20yrs old and thinks she has a clue. I am not and do not, but something in the way I am looking at her is making her blush and say, 'You bad man'. If thinking about fucking her tight little ass is bad, then I have to agree. I tell her, whispering in her ear and her face gets very red, but she does not look away. This is a good sign. She kisses me goodnight as we all say goodbye.

The next day she visits me at work and we eat together. Some kids I teach later have seen her and laugh about 'my friend', 'is she your girlfriend'? 'Gik', I say, meaning number 2 girlfriend.

They do not know she is a ladyboy. I am relieved, as I don't want that particular conversation with a group of 14 year olds!

Focus begins sending me sms messages that begin with 'why you not call', and end with, 'I love you, I miss you so much'. There is no middle ground with ladyboys!

The next time we meet she is getting her nails done elaborately and wearing a dress that displays her new tits particularly well. She is proud of them. I am a big fan. She says, 'what you want do?' I say, 'You want go to a hotel?' 'Really, really, she says, you want?'

'Yes, I do!' We are miles from Nana or Patpong where rooms for the purpose of fucking are easily found so we ask the taxi driver as we motivate down Ladprao road. We find a seedy short time for 350 baht but I tell her it's not good enough for her and we go to a regular hotel next door and for 495 baht we have a room fit for purpose.

It is so easy to find Ladyboys in this city and not only prostitutes. Regular ladyboys are not so different from their working sisters; they all want a farang for money, security, sex, status and maybe love and that's a fact, take it to the bank.

We kiss for a long time and her body is perfect. Then she flexes her long, smooth, tan, asian legs to let me enter her. It is hot, raw and wet down there but I will not flinch. She is not at all coy. That is a very good thing.

While I was fucking Focus an SMS from Farida arrived. 'I go to see customer'. Half an hour later I am at Phra Rama 9 MRT station and I see the road where she is meeting a half Korean kid who works as an engineer on the BTS in Bangkok. I am sitting drinking a cold beer in the Gran Mercure hotel lobby and listening to some polite violin music when she arrives. 3000 baht for 40 minutes work. My girl's fast! Farida bought us cocktails and we got a bit drunk together. We played a game of insulting each other as elaborately as possible on my part and on hers, well when you have heard a Thai ladyboy call you a chuntch (cunt) or an asshooole or 'shlutman' or heard her say, 'I fuchk your mother bischt', and 'I fuck your bischt ashoole', a few times, elaboration is no longer necessary. Her accent makes everything bad she says sound funny. I am her proud teacher! She is incomparable.

Miss Hi-So and anyone one or anything else is so easily forgotten when I am with her. She makes me happy in so many ways.

Another cocktail hour follows her meeting with another customer the next day at the A Hotel on Sathorn. She massaged him and fucked his ass while dressed as a University girl. He was done in 20 minutes. 3000 baht again sounds like easy money? Think again. Finding his asshole was difficult as it seems he was rather larger than expected. 'He owain mack, David'!

Farida won't fuck me, not that I am too concerned. 'I am queen and you are King', she says. It would fuck up her fragile sense of self-image that imagines herself as a woman. She and other ladyboys fuck customers who want it, for the money. Gate told me the same thing. What they really want is to be treated and fucked like women. Some ladyboys are contrary to this. Some love fucking men. I have met a few and they all have a predatory look in their eyes when you get up close. They give me a sense of how a woman feels when talking to a horny man . . .excited, scared, desired but definitely hunted! Of course Ladyboys like that usually accompany the look in their eyes with some choice English phrases whispered in your ear, 'I can fuck you good, make It so not hurt, you want? I knowing you want.' Try that in an English provincial nightclub, give the doormen a laugh as they throw you out.

Farida wastes my waking hours with impunity. She is not old enough to understand the cruelty of fleeting time or measure the heavy hand of ages passed. She is just what I need if only I can listen to her song as we lay in one another's arms a little longer.

At the sound of her voice, the salmon-falls and whatever is begotten, born, and will die turns in that sensual music of Yeats imagination. I must, like those beautiful souls, neglect the monuments of intellect. I cannot think on it more. I cannot reason, only feel, or I will kill this beautiful, strange creature called love that has grown up between us. When she stands close to me I lose all reason, all doubt, all despair. She calls me on my way home from work. She is meeting a customer on soi 11. I tell her I will wait for her close by. I get off the MRT at Asoke and drink a beer outside the Thermae coffee shop. I watch the life of the city flow past my bottle. Think. An SMS to tell me the room number, the hotel, the name to keep her safe. I wait, drink. Another SMS 30 minutes later. 'I come now, where are you?' I reply, 'Meet you outside the hotel baby'. As I walk down 11 she calls me, 'Dawid, come here, customer not pay me', her voice is thick, choking. I walk into the lobby, ignore security and find the elevator. At the room and I knock. She opens the door. She is talking fast and a white guy in his shorts moves from deep in the room towards me. It happens fast now and I knock him back into the room. He stumbles back heavily like a drunk, making space between us. 'He not pay what he say, give me only 1200baht and he make video and not pay extra like he say'. The American is subdued now, careful, scared. I know violence is not necessary. He tells me she took money from his jacket hanging on a chair. 'Only 300 baht you owe me', she says. He uses my name, 'David, she is lying, she stole from me and she took the video'. 'Because you wanna take my face so I hold camera' she says.

I say, 'Pay her the money'. He says, 'I don't have it' fumbling in his clothes. 'Pay her now'. I am short on words. Conversation is flowing around me. I concentrate on him, listen to her. She gives me the camera and I supervise the deletion of the video that shows her body, her brown tits, him fucking her, his mouth hovering over her cock as she comes in fast forward mode. She was holding the camera. I am dispassionate. He opens the safe and takes a handful of big notes out. He is a fool. For a moment I consider taking it all; his camera, money and laptop. The moment passes. He tries to reason with me in his fear, to tell me in familiar tones of shared ethnicity that she is being unfair. This, for only 300 baht and an undisclosed sum promised for the video. I tell him, 'she does not tell lies'. He asks me to choose his version of the truth as a fellow farang pitted against a foreigner. I leave with my foreigner and only what money she is owed. Back on the street we stand with our backs to the neon, pinned under the rolling, adolescent

Bangkok sky. 'Only one thing is sure', I say; 'we will not grow old'. I tell her to avoid disputes next time and never to take money even if she believes she has the right. She nods in compliance, stares at me. Her breasts are heaving. Adrenalin does that to a body. She reaches for my hand. I take it in mine. Her eyes shine and she tells me, 'I want you be my boyfriend always'. 'Ok', I say, choosing her.

Book Two

Ladyboys
The inside story

When the sun dies and the hot winds blow you to desolation and the tourists are gone there is little hope and nothing to anticipate. The smouldering autumn sinks through Sukhumvit and my heart is hollow and dry and as empty as the soi 4 bars. She is gone. Not with a dramatic flourish as finale to this most memorable, most painful love affair but with a slow fading out.

One. Black Magic and Barbie

There is nothing culturally oblique about the dingy corridor leading to her apartment. It stinks and reeks of inner city deprivation.

Even as you sit bare-arsed on the rubber covered mattress you make excuses; you imagine momentarily that what you sense as dirty, dingy and depressing has other significance because this is Thailand, a third world country. You are not buying it.

The place is startlingly barren of anything that could bear being appended by the adjective, comfortable.

The person who lives here just carries herself as if she does not see what you see. As you watch, she moves her hands just so and fixes in place the eye, the earring a beauty spot on the soulless, chilling face of a doll.

Those hands had handled your body with equal dexterity only minutes earlier.

You are fascinated and appalled by what directs those hands. She seems to posses an older intelligence that inhabits another world, another culture entirely and interacts with the world with another gendered attention. The atmosphere in the room is made more surreal by the smoke that curls and drifts its way into your memory.

You cannot express even in thoughts the precise reason you are there. Perhaps it is because you are searching for some wisdom. Perhaps an insight into the Thai mind, the Thai ladyboy mind but you know it is more than this. You need something. You need some kind of release or closure and you have been searching for it for what seems a long time. You have searched for it in the eyes and bodies of the ladyboys. You did not find it there.

Your story is far from unique but you want to be a survivor. Maybe you are looking for an exorcism.

You will remember only impressions of this night. The details are obscured by something altogether outside of your experience.

You know the answer. You are in the presence of the mystical.

The air is different inside this room. She does not speak for long periods of time. She wears no make-up tonight because of course you are not paying for the skin she wears at that rocky promontory into Sukhumvit and the farang world; Cascades, but her breasts, ass, skin and mouth have been alluring enough. Her scarred chest is difficult to look at. A knife attack in the dark soi and a robbery seem too simple an explanation and you suspect a darker version of events in which she is not the only victim.

As she works and talks in her slurred, Khmen, black magic, rambling, spell- like chit-chat you are remembering a Nigerian pilot and his wife who rented a flat from your father. They turned the fire onto its back and cooked sausages and pieces of meat over the electric bars. The shanty-town was still in them even in that big, foreign city. Thai people from the hinterlands of Isaan do not really adjust to Bangkok city living. They just make their surroundings more familiar. They are still sitting cross-legged on a dirt floor eating Bala even when they are really in Ratchada or Thonglor or Ekkamai.

She tells you about the blood that women from Buriram and Surin put in their boyfriend's drinking water to make them fall in love. You think about John and Ploy and her obsession with him, her jealousy, her desire, her primitive love for him and her power. You think about fighting cocks, card games and motorcycle accident wounds on brown legs. The marks of the Khmen.

J rambles on, slurring her words. She is suspended from Cascades by the mama-san for fighting. Her New Year will be bleak unless she finds some customers. She hopes you may become her boyfriend but there is something too ancient and earthy about her. She rattles off the names of the ladyboys she knows who have black magic power and are able to attract lots of customers. She tells you that she too could place a spell on her lips so that when you kiss her you will not forget but be compelled to come back to her.

You are thinking about Farida and how you have tried so hard and for so long to get her out of your blood. Did you drink hers?

'I never saw her do anything like black magic', you tell J. She laughs at you, 'That is because she is a Khmen witch. Why you not know dat'?

Suddenly, you believe in black magic. J begins to tell you about the mafia and how because she saved the life of one of them, she has their allegiance. She tells you about her white magic and how she is untouchable. She tells you other things too difficult to hear and impossible to tell. She knows you can see them. She tells you way too much.

That's when you leave.

Two. Last Shot in the Dark Soul

She used to tell me, 'Balloons are like lovers, once you let them go you can never get them back'. She never listened to her own advice.

In your apartment the afternoon sun makes a kaleidoscope of dust and dark, Asian hair on the cold, faux marble floor. You sit alone on your unmade bed and you think again of Farida. You have not been 'together' like before for a month or more but you see her every day. You just can't seem to say goodbye to each other but something is dying, departing. You can feel it leaving, making its last sad goodbyes. It won't return. You know this feeling and the monumental sadness that replaces love in your heart.

You cry a little but say the words, 'mai longhai', 'I not cry', to yourself like a mantra. The words are a knot of grass at the cliff's edge; the only thing left between you and the abyss.

May calls and asks you if you wanna come over to Ratchada, drink some beer, smoke cigarettes together and fuck. When you say you cannot come her voice leaves a silence that you cannot fill. You don't have words left. When the door closes behind lovers what is left? Silent, empty air before you occupy your mind and body with another distraction. Love is gone. Only its traces and a handful of snapshot memories are left behind to compensate for its loss.

The ordinary world bears down on you as that magical thing called love breathes its last beautiful, heartbreaking breath.

Rest now. Tell your heart to rest. It's all over. Love has left the building. Her clothes and her shoes are still by the door. Love has run careless through your life never knowing the indelible marks she leaves with her smile, her laughter, her hugs and her touch. How could she know? She is ageless and immortal now in your memory.

Today is the last time you will meet her.

A child watches the river at Taksin Bridge boil with fish. They are inedible and hence, in abundance.

The sky begins to roll moodily. King Rama the Third accepts blessings impassively. Will the flood come? A half built deserted riverside condominium slides into decay; is it a sign, a portent of things to come? She is walking ahead of me, almost out of sight; out of reach. My heart and hands won't stretch any further.

Is this love or the waiting before it dies? What do we want? Why are we here? I feel like I am in mourning.

The Rooster on the Chinese temple swivels an eye towards me, its totem bearer. I need some direction but the train leaves as we mount the darkening stairs from Thonburi. Things are departing today, fleeing the city.

A gentle, Thai tailor grasps my hand as he always does as I walk past him on the narrow channel from soi 6 to Krungthonburi road. He smiles, shakes his head a little. What does he know of me and the six-foot kathoey who matches my stride. Enough, I think.

The monk watching from the temple steps has an air of empathy too. What does it mean? His companions are busy making credit and phone calls.

The air of expectancy is febrile, contagious but one man is not touched by the world. He is not a monk but his tattoos seem to speak of service and hard use of some kind. He feeds the birds with a surprising gentleness and joy.

The traffic rushes past the billboards advertising the 'white diet', quick money and overpriced condos. Most of the passengers just need a place to sleep for the night, maybe in Pattaya.

The last photograph I took of Farida is of the girl I fell in love with and whom I will never be able to forget. I know now that nothing will ever be resolved between us. No answers will ever be furnished to ease my heart. 'Did she ever love me', will remain a satellite orbiting what remains of my life and will travel with me to every corner of this city. Every hotel in which she met customers, every bar I waited for her, every soi that is peopled by prostitutes and every ladyboy I ever see will, in my imagination, whisper that question. 'Well, did she'? But the photograph shows only a lonely ladyboy trapped between the stars and the earth, her family and her beauty, love and money. I want to weep for her in her loneliness, and mine.

She asked me to go with her to the Pukow Tong festival.

I am sure she never believed I would really leave her. Sometimes I still cannot believe I did. Was that the single biggest mistake in my life or an escape to freedom and some kind of peace? I swear I still don't know. I am filled with regret and longing still when I look at her picture on that night.

Just like fairs in provincial England, Pukow Tong was full of teenagers out together, laughing, eating and drinking out of sight of the family. Unlike England, large groups of teenage ladyboys were amongst the throng. I tried to shake a stick at them but there were too many and anyway they were all shaking their own sticks, figuratively speaking. We ate and laughed but she held a tension behind her eyes. We played carnival games and the big wheel turned and prayers were said for those departed souls, missed and loved. She insisted I try to win a prize for her. A calm possessed me as I shot at the painted target.

I watched as a family sent love and luck to a dead relative through the water as it poured from jug to bowl and as those nearby reached out and sent their energy to join with his on its journey.

I think something bitter also passed with the water.

Perhaps it is true, as Thais believe that the spirit can be passed through water. If love can be sent to a dead relative, maybe pain can be washed away, cleansed from the spirit.

Something happened to me that night. Something happened that changed my life. My heart became strong enough to say goodbye with love.

So I did.

Three. Waking up

She is dancing out there on the edge of your waking mind, defying reason, logic and good sense. Young, naïve, beautiful and possessing of a kind of happy, untutored wisdom and warmth you crave more with every day that she is gone.

Annie, where are you and why did I ever let you go?

You wake up and roll onto your back, a little bit wiser than in the days that have gone before. The room spins past your eyes just like the last months in Bangkok; recognisable as days but lacking any real definition; a hazy semblance of time passing and ladyboys passing through. You wipe the wetness from your eyes and feel a curved, smooth shaft pressing into your side. So smooth it feels like brown ivory. She mumbles; 'Tahan', in her bleary slumber.

The radio is still playing from last night's whisky a go-go in your loom but in the light of day the music is more portentous than it has any right to be.

The cold blast of the air conditioner that you have never got around to adjusting begins to wake you up. It's fucking unpleasant.

You do not even have the distraction of May's body to occupy your tumbling mind; she won't be awake for hours yet. It is only 11am and she lives in a different time zone from us working stiffs.

So put me on a highway, show me a sign.

And take it to the limit one more time.

The music fades as you remember . . . Five weeks earlier:

'When we go into the apartment lobby, if I tell you, go to the toilet and wait until I call you to come out Annie, ok?'

'Ok, I go, but not need pee-pee'. 'It not matter, ok, just waiting me there baby'. Earlier that day you had toured the condos in the vicinity looking for a suitable swimming hole/party venue. Your apartment does not have a pool so you have to visit friends of which you have precious few or con your way into a hotel or condominium. Q house presented the best opportunity and you had crossed the Thai security guards palm with silver. Now she love you long time sure. Farangs are rarely challenged.

She throws up a little salute as you enter the lobby with Annie trotting along beside you; faithful, adorable little Annie.

What a cheap asshole you are.

'Bring your swimming clothes, I take you to pool party', you told

126

Annie this morning. Excited she arrived looking delicious and ready to be devoured by you, the guy she wants to be her boyfriend.

The inner door to the elevators is closed and of course you don't have a key card but anticipating this you push Annie towards the toilet and wait. You smile too many times at the receptionists and pace, waiting for a real resident to open the door that you then hold open, call Annie and enter.

The pool is on the top floor and you swim luxuriously in the Bangkok heat and ignore Annie studiously.

What a fucking idiot you were.

She comes and sits by you, follows you around the pool adoringly, smiles and laughs hysterically, as do you, when a little Thai boy cannot stop laughing out loud at his cartoon book.

This beautiful, special day that you failed to recognise as such could have been the start of something wonderful.

You felt something more for her than lust on that day and that is why you were so cool with her.

Sad, sad fool.

Twisted up with the lies and the double, trouble Ladyboy drama you have lived with for so long, you recognised that the feeling of sabai-jai you have when you are with her could grow into something that can hurt you as well as make you feel good. So you hid from her.

What a fucking disappointment you were.

In all your lust, you never took her anywhere. You never made her feel special or gave her more than a 100baht note for her taxi home. What a mistake you made. You never told her you loved her and now she's gone to Pattaya to find an old friend.

Annie's family all worked in construction. They lived together, uncles, brothers, sisters on soi 27, Punnawithi, on a building site. When the Thais work on a new apartment building they construct a kind of tin city and live inside it for the duration of the job. The first time she asked me to go and meet her family it was raining hard. She stepped daintily across the muddy ruts and puddles outside the giant shack she was calling home. Inside I sat on her bed: a plywood board wedged between two upright timbers and the side of the corrugated tin wall. Everyone else slept on the hard floor.

We sat with the men, girls and babies and played 'HI-LO', a kind of Thai roulette but with dice not a wheel. Big money was won and lost, whisky was shared and that sense of 'live today, don't think too much something will turn up tomorrow', was as palpable, as breathable as the cigarette smoke that filled the room.

I took her home. I wish I had kept her there but I let her go back to that place the next day; and the next, and next until I stopped calling her and she gave up on me.

You met a few weeks ago, at the end of July. It was a Facebook assignation.

In her friend's room at Phra Kanong, Annie kept her clothes in a shopping bag. You thought nothing of it then only seeing her eyes and her smile.

She invited you there one Sunday afternoon.

Riding down Suk 44, Ekkamai on the moto your stomach is contracting into a knot, 'maybe this girl, maybe someone to take away the pain?' She comes downstairs and watches you climb from the pillion. The knot tightens; she is beautiful. She is wearing a little, red T-shirt and denim shorts. Her long hair is curling a little in bangs that fall to her shoulder. She is very beautiful. You smile.

As you followed her up the apartment stairs she said, 'My friend stay here is ok?' It was OK. Anything she said was OK.

Her friend was sitting in between two mattresses on the floor watching gay porn on her Iphone. You stopped like hitting a wall. Her friend was Ice of Guess Bar, perhaps the only Ladyboy in Bangkok you truly dislike. She is a miserable bitch who's meanness is barely concealed by the 'Yim me lessanai', (the smile that masks wicked thoughts). Like King Richard the Third, this ladyboy could smile while murdering babies.

Annie stretched her lean body out on the bed opposite you and made small talk in Ladyboyenglish, a nod, a smile a word or two.

'You look good Anne', you say, sitting on the highest of the beds. 'Yingwa', sneers Ice. (This word means 'more than' in Thai, ladyboys use this to compliment each other, meaning 'you are more beautiful than a real woman'.)

Ice is being sarcastic.

'You horny' says the hideous Ice sitting between you like a goblin. 'I horny too, but everyone must pay'.

The idea of a threesome that had been running through your dirty mind (despite your dislike of Ice) stops in its tracks.

Then the goblin says to Annie, 'You horny, can boom-boom, I not shy'. Annie sits by your side and touches your leg. You hear cracked wedding bells and suddenly see her dressed in white. Shaking that out of your mind you are about to leave when your future wife says, 'You want to meet later?'

A hymn from your schooldays plays through your mind; 'All things bright and beautiful, the Lord God made them all'.

As you climb on the back of a moto, your legs are shaking. 'Home James', you think with a smile.

The days pass and you have been with her, to the mall, the movies, the bedroom and every minute is spent smiling and laughing. You have spent so little money on her but she tells you. 'It ok, I have money before but no happy, I only need little to take care.' Doubting her words you talk to her friend,

'Some people not care too mush about money only want someone love them'. Annie is like soul food for a jaded heart. She happily teaches you Thai phrases and laughs at your attempts to reproduce the tones correctly; 'narak', she says, thinking your foolishness cute. You tell her she is too young to be your girlfriend that this is only fun for a short time that she is free to do whatever she wants whenever she wants. You see that twist like a knife in her guts but she says nothing, except, 'you think easy find someone take care my heart?' But you are too lost in the past to see the shining, bright present unfold before your eyes. You don't understand why you call her less and less.

Four. Five Easy Pieces or 'Am I Gay, Romeo?'

Sunday: Arika

Sometimes it seems to you that Bangkok is ordering your life, spinning events like plates that you struggle to balance. Bangkok has denied you love and made you suffer at the hands of the Khmen witch Farida. You have no love in your heart now. Your one chance, your possible saviour, your little angel, Annie is gone. You do not think about your reasons for not calling her.

There is something else you must do.

Now you will be the bad man everyone thinks you are. You will give them hell. Liars beware.

'Just watch me', you whisper to yourself as you wait for Arika who foolishly says she wants to meet you at BTS Krungthonburi station.

You wait like a killer by the 7/11 feeling beautifully depraved having finally found a kind of symmetry. In truth, you have retreated, made your heart hard. The Thais call it, Jai damn. (black heart)

Your revenge tragedy unfolds. Act one arrives on smooth legs and black high heels. She is so small she bounces along, holding your hand as you lead her to the place of taxation. You are imagining the havoc you will wreak on her small, slim ladyboy body.

She has some idea of the shit that is about to go down but not the bitter seed you are carrying in your toxic heart. There should be skull and crossbones on your chest and the word, 'Toxic' stencilled in black letters. This cargo has to be dumped.

There is little talking in the loom. Talking is superfluous when the heat is on and in your bodies. You are animals now. Her chest is featureless and smooth, her cock is long and polished like the branch of a tree. Her mouth is open and she inhales you. You take time punishing her for her beauty. She comes first and then starts screaming for you to stop or come, either will do. You are in no rush. Let the bitch scream. Her contorted face gives you a dark satisfaction. There is nothing beautiful about this coupling, no afterglow, no loving embrace. You make it clear you want her to go, mumbling something about getting up early. Sadly, the more you withdraw the more she comes on like a teenager, like you are the first person to fuck her. She's Bangkok crazy. After she leaves you check the emails from your newly discovered hook up site.

'Planet Romeo', is a less obviously 'gay' offshoot of 'Gay Romeo' but you still get 101 messages from gay men who 'want to fuck you so much'. Still, there is gold in them thar hills amongst the butt ugly boulders.

Monday: After dinner Mint.

A younger version of Arika but much tougher, Mint is stripping off her dress as she steps into your room and you follow her to the bed. You push her down onto her knees and your cock into her mouth.

Even as you watch her sucking, a Khmen voice echoes through the chambers of your head, 'I never come your dirty loom again Dawid, you cannot stop fucking them in the ass you like so much.'

You are on a mission to prove the voice right. How many ladyboys can you fuck for free in one week? Mint comes and goes. It's hard to remember her face. She moaned a lot in pain when you fucked her. You felt nothing. Sweet.

Tuesday: Maggie Q.

Maggie's picture is ultra-feminine and pretty. She says she is tall and wants to meet on a soi near Ekkamai. The motosyc drops you at the 7. You call her, say you are waiting. You smoke a cigarette and look around numbly at the Thai faces on motosycs, bikes and carts rushing past like a moving watercolour. Then suddenly you sense someone there at your shoulder.

You are shocked at her height. She is easily 6ft 2in in flat shoes. Her dark hair is tied back and she has too much white powder on her face. She says we have to pay for a room because she stays with her friend.

400 baht later you are together in a bedroom and it's about to happen. Kissing her is exciting even though she feigns some kind of shyness. Maybe she is shy. You get naked and her skin is slick with sweat. The room is hot. She has a flat chest and a big cock. She has let down her hair now but her jaw is angular, long and masculine. So is her body. You have more than a moment of disequilibrium. A voice inside your head is telling you that 'she' is a guy, a fucking guy. 'What are you doing', the voice says, 'just get the fuck out of here, you don't want this anyway', but your libido isn't listening. While she showers you devise your plan to escape scot free.

None of these ladyboys ask for money on the phone or in emails. If indeed they want money they are being less than honest. You tell them all you are looking for a girlfriend. This is true in a fucked up Bangkok kind of way. Before meeting you are filled with nervous anticipation and your blood is on fire with electricity that you can almost see burning through your veins and arteries and all culminating in your cock. You are searching for the one who keeps that fire burning. Again you are searching. Pre-empting Maggie's possible request for money you ask her what she is doing later in the week. She tells you that she is a student at Khon Kaen University.

The Thai volleyball team is losing to Slovenia on the hotel room TV and Maggie tells you she plays for her university. 'Team sow-sow', you ask hopefully? 'Num-num', she says and stares at you as your mouth drops open. She plays for the university men's team! You feel a cold, wet ripple down your back and head for the door. You chew gum as you walk up the crowded soi looking for a motosyc. The sky is getting dark and you have to be Mr. Clean at work for a few hours pretending you are in Thailand for the culture, 'Oh Yeh, and the food, the fucking food'.

Wednesday: MJ and Lin.

MJ is arriving at 9pm. You have to go out and buy some shaving gel, razors and some other sundry bullshit before she arrives. MJ has a kinda elfin thing going on for her. Her teeth are braced with brightly coloured stops. Only in Thailand could a painful dental procedure become a fashion accessory. She looks young in her photos but nothing is gonna stop her coming over to your dirty room.

The floods have reduced the availability of many things including shaving gel so you take a sky ride to Taksin and a subterranean grocery store ironically named, 'Topps'. In the aisle you see a lank and shapely figure that is a cross between supermodel feminine and athletic boy. She is a young Amazonian. She is walking away from you as you follow her up the noodle aisle. She is wearing tiny denim shorts and a tight, red Tee. She has reddish brown hair and her bra strap is visible through the Tee.

She stops to answer a phone call and so you browse. Moments later the phone call ends and she is crying.

When you ask her what's wrong she tells you in Tinglish that her little sister of 14 is pregnant. You murmur something to the effect of things turning out ok and not to worry. She grabs your hand and takes you to show you her picture of Buddha in her loom so you can pray together. She leads you across the soi and up a rat-infested part of Bangkok that the tourists never see. You have never felt so depressed and were it not for the hard on growing in your pants you would have chickened out. But Lin is pretty and unexpected. The stairs to her room are dirty and populated by cats, cockroaches, rats and children playing together in a game called poverty.

In her room you kiss and the warm orange glow from a light-bulb behind bug paper becomes romantic. She pulls away from the kiss too quickly though and takes off her shirt. She has no breasts at all but her smooth skin and her ass are enough. You cup one ass cheek in the palm of your hand until she sits down on a crappy weave chair and on cue, you drop your pants. She is sucking now with deep, slow gulps and your brain stops working well. 'You can give me little bit money', she asks, looking up at you.

Before you can stop it you hear the word, 'No', coming from you mouth. 'But why', says your cock, 'what's the problem', give her 500 baht and fuck her'.

You will not bend. You did so much bending when you were with the Farida that you bent out of shape. No more. Sex and money do not mix. Not now. Not ever again. No more. Instead you pull up your pants, tell Lin you have to go and promise to call her knowing you never will. The reptile part of you knows that MJ is on her way. Sometimes you think yourself a cheap asshole hiding behind a principle.

MJ is too delicious. She is like an exotic fruit that has begun to perish in the sun. So much sweet juice that does not have long before it hardens into a sticky inedible goo. Maybe that explains the speed of her actions. You want to eat her face but she is all business and for that she must pay. Her ass is tight and like a peach. You penetrate her without mercy and although she is hurting you don't stop. She just grimaces and urges you on. It's almost as if she is in a hurry. She is. You offer her nothing and she asks for a little money. You know she is going to Nana to work the street and so you give her 100 baht for the fare. She took herself off the girlfriend short-list when she stopped kissing you and rushed to the next step; boom-boom, it's over. You see MJ later that year on Nana. You miss her just a little in a Bangkok kind of 'missing you', way: Sentimental, Fictional.

Friday: Ploy

You decide you are going to void the warranty with Ploy. She has the softly chiselled features of an internet goddess. Her beautiful vulnerability makes you want to hurt her. You know you are a bad person.

She has been away to see her family and you have waited for her because she is so schoolgirl sexy. She is at university in Rangsit and Rangsit is very far away. You have measured your desire before committing time, energy and money into dating this girl. She speaks so well, is so gorgeous and wants you to go to her room. Finally you can resist no longer and catch a taxi into the moonless night's inky book. You are going to write in it with your cock.

240baht and a thought space later you find yourself standing under a street lamp next to a squid cart. The squid seller looks at you knowingly. She knows that a farang out in the suburban hinterland after 10pm is up to no good. Ploy tells you she, 'come in 2 minute, she have to make face good.'

She comes from the apartment behind you and she looks better than the pictures. She is a young beauty queen waiting to be despoiled. A voice whispering inside of you is excited about that job.

The room is hot and so is she. She apologises for the non-existent sweat under her armpits. I tell her I want to lick them and I do, peeling her pants down until she has only a damp T-shirt on her body. Her long cock is darker than the rest of her body.

She puts on some music. You kiss and move together in something like a dance although you barely move because what matters is not the dance but the heat of her body on yours. That matters a lot. Her cock is surprising; strong and thick. She wants to get on the bed but you hold her close and kiss her like a drunken bear eating honey.

You want to feel her body now; her hips, her home-grown breasts pressed against you for the first time together in this dance. Her smell is scalding, burning your nostrils. You are both wet and the heat is palpable. You want to drink her smell, her soap and the scent in her hair. She moves to the window and lets in some air that carries her stink to your nostrils like the spore of a little fox to a downwind tracker. The stars are bright and the hunting is good.

She presses against you and strips her T-shirt. The hollow of her throat is moist and tastes like wine in your mouth.

The violence of your big dogs, thrusting, careless, dark body makes her pale fragility transcendent and intoxicating. As you look down on her shuddering beauty as she is spread before you on the dark blue counterpane of her bed, you feel complete. Your big-lump cock in her angelic mouth makes you complete. Why are you so sick?

She makes a phone call and the heady music that was playing inside your fuckoxicated brain screeches to a stop. She is talking in rapid fire tinglish to an unknown friend who has a farang boyfriend. She speaks in snatches with big breaths in between just long enough to keep living. A strange feeling is growing inside your heart as she grasps your wrist preventing you from getting up.

'I want you talk my friend's boyfriend', she says in a voice like a pissed off baby. You pull your arm free and stand up. The wakening signs of dangerous revenge move across her face and her lips curl cruelly; now she looks like an angry piglet with a flick knife set of nails. 'Why', you say, holding your breath. 'I want she know I boyfriend more than she and good looking more than she because, because, (deep breath) because, I beauty more than she'. The phone rings again and it is reported that the boyfriend is not available as he is 'away'? You listen to Ploy's creole of English and Thai as she fantasises about you to her friend. You hear handsome, big, (breath) and 'big cock'. You hear the age 26, and know she is mad.

She is talking about you to 'lift up' her status. Thai people want to possess 'lift- up' power; money, education, farang boyfriends. You begin to feel like an accessory. It's time to go.

You have no idea how to get home. It's 1am and black as pitch. The stars have gone to sleep and you want to emulate them now that the magic has gone. Ploy is Lady Macbeth mad. She dresses and you to wait for her to show you where to catch a motosyc or a taxi.

A voice from the bathroom, 'Dahling, I just to buy a new shirt for university tomorrow can you give to me 600 baht, dahling'? You tell her you have only enough money for the taxi. She says,' why you bring only small money, why dahling, why?' You think she is going to escalate in her craziness but you tell her, 'I meet you later and buy shirt ok?' 'Ok, dahling!' In the taxi you reflect. 'Freedom', and 'Free' are words you like very much. But in a portent of things to come the Baiyoke Tower is a shining blade against the Bangkok skyline.

You have never seen her again.

Five. Prisoners of the Spectacle

You have become a Facebook Romeo. This is the latest manifestation of your lonely, haunted heart. The brain breeds trouble for those who throw caution to the wind. Trouble arrives with a capital 'C', for Cascades. The slave girls are calling from their rocky island where they are forced to suck the cocks of any passing pirate from England, Switzerland or the Americas.

June adds you. She has a mouth so big that when she tells you that her father is Ugandan, you believe her immediately. 'Oooy,' she says, 'narak, you believe me Dawid'. She is amused by your naivety. Charmed you tell her to sit next to you on the big sofa. You have just finished eating in Central World's food court and you have barely been able to drag your eyes away from her big breasts and her killer smile. She is a walking, talking advertisement for sex tourism. They should put her ass in the ads.

She is not a number! Although, she has one on her bikini when she dances at Cascades. 'I want a girlfriend, I not pay for you June', despite this information and your obvious lust, she wants to meet you and now she is curling herself against you and purring through that big Siamese smile and those big Siamese eyes. She is hotter than a tumbling dice. 'Where we go now?' she asks. 'We can go my room', she says. 'You want', she says. 'Up to you', I say (heartbeat) 'We can go', she says, smiling. You have learned to say little and do less in these situations, at least until the moment of truth. Sex for money is the game these girls play. Meeting you, knowing that you will not pay for sex is a gamble on their part. Or maybe just lust.

Welcome to the greatest quiz show on Earth.

When a ladyboy agrees to meet you what is she thinking?

Now you are laying on her bed next to another of the slave girls who shares her room in Ekkamai. She has a new tattoo, you like the way it feels; proud of

her olive, oiled leg. You are daydreaming about women's prisons. What would it be like; being passed around by the inmates?

June comes back from the 'Seben' with supplies and stands smiling at you. You stand eye to eye with her and she grins like a crazy Cherokee cat. She takes a big hard cock from her shorts and puts it in your hand. You are naked in 4 seconds flat. 4 seconds later she's pushing the back of your head lower onto the same massive cock that of course is attached to her taut lower abdomen. 60 seconds after that you are copying that action as it seemed like fun. It is. Her 'namwow' hits her in the face and shoulder as you fuck her.

Life is good. Life is sweet but about to get complicated. Complicated, as only telling the truth can get complicated.

As you fly up 23 on the back of a tiny moto the mad professor calls you. Meet, drink, accepted. It's 7pm in Nana and you are sitting next to 'Obsessions'. The Prof is talking way too much and what's worse he's talking way too much in Thai. You tell him that at this clip he has no hope of ever getting laid, especially as he is using his superannuated linguistic skill to complain about his soon to be ex-girlfriend.

Only one course of action will silence him, so you take him to Casanova, a wild and crazy ladyboy bar that you know well.

'Are you sure they are ALL really Ladyboys'? He asks me and every 'girl' in the joint at least four times. Finally, after it has to be said, he has bought drinks for everyone, Nadia shouts, 'ALL' in his face and stalks off. I watch him fall instantly in love with her and wonder if I have done a good thing or a very, very bad one?

Six. Down with the Numbers

The seasons begin to run backwards; first it was June and then, just like that, May came around.

The night does strange things to a man . . . these feelings, maybe you can understand.

The bar is full of dark sounds and light and June is shrinking out of sight. May is dancing and the world holds its breath.

I hope I don't fall in love with you as you dance up there for me to see But it's clear that you are lonely just like me.

Falling in love just makes me sad and blue but the only perfect thing around is you.

You, You, You, number 22.

I'll have another drink or three because as you dance you display your heart for me to see.

I hope I don't fall in love with you.

But when you smile at me I think we could make it, Break the jinx and take it somewhere cool and green far from the barrooms crowded scene. It remains to be seen how I can extricate myself from your mate. I think she's great and I saw you just a day too late to show you I am hot and shot away by you, I mean for real, that's what I feel.

This is not some superficial lust that must be fed by your lips and your hips and what hangs there like the leg of a chair.

I don't care about your cock and maybe that's a shock but true from me to you number 22. Now you sit by me and drink a drink bought by our friend while I pretend not to care while I look at your hair and touch your skin. Whichever way I look I cannot win.

What I'm trying to say, May, is that I hope I don't fall in love with you my beautiful, shimmering, big breasted, gentle, voracious, number 22. It happens in a beat or two.

June takes the Prof and I upstairs to Cascades where she pays her bar-fine to the ogre under the waterfall and we have a drink or two.

May (working name), number 22, or Jak (Thai nickname) is dancing and looking at me as if lust could kill while June sits by my side.

Something happens to my heart.

I talk to May for an hour. We are one and the same person, flesh folding in on itself, eyes eating each other's features. We cannot touch. It is perfect.

Much later when the Prof has gone home and the moon has given up on us, I eat with all the numbers, May, Sai, June, Bee, Toei and others deep somewhere in the early morning soi. May tries to swop numbers with June, reading hers aloud so I can hear but June spots the ruse and tells her to 'poot Thai, mai Angritt', so I won't understand.

It is hard to watch May's form shrink into the dawn as the taxi takes me in the wrong direction home.

I sent June an SMS message the next day because in a world of liars I decide to make a stand. I make a choice to be different. I am 'Falang'.

'June, I hope you are not angry. I tell you because I respect you and not want to lie. You know I met your friend (May) last night and I like her too much. I want to see her again. Sorry.' June replied:

'Here is her number ******* not speak with me again Dawid. Goodbye forever.'

Free now I reflect on ladyboys love of drama. June and I spent only three days together so is the drama, the jealousy and the possessiveness merely smoke produced to hide the truth; the economic imperative that inspires them to bind themselves to us. Smoke to cover the long con? The girlfriend 'experience' that is just an experience; a fitful, dramatic bout of exciting weather produced backstage by a poorly paid stagehand with a wobbly board and a watering can? Smoke to make us believe their lies? Sure it is.

May and I meet. I tell her I want a girlfriend not a whore and that means I won't pay. She tells me that I paid for June. 'No, I gave her one thousand baht to pay her bar-fine and make face by buying drinks for her friends. She never asked for money and I will not pay for sex, so, it's up to you', I tell her.

We spent the weekend making love, talking and laughing at photos, just like normal people. She likes Victorian and Edwardian clothing. I show her some stage costume of the period and she sees a photo of my young self when I was a soldier.

She falls in love with the young me. Irony was never sharper. The young me could never love a ladyboy. The older me loves them too much.

So she loves my younger self, my ghost. She makes love to the soldier, the 'Tahan' I once was. She is possessed and we are having sex again when the door I forgot to lock opens and in walks Farida.

I bustle her back outside and she spends 30 minutes begging me to come outside and speak with her while May hides her face under the covers.

Finally I do.

She is hurt that I chose to not wait for her to come back from Singapore or Nana or Pattaya or some other family-financing prostitution excursion she was in the process of undertaking when last we spoke. I tell her she has no right to be angry, not after she broke the rules so badly, running off to Pattaya with a customer for 15,000 baht. This time I tell her to go.

May and I spend the rest of the weekend pretending we could be lovers, knowing we never will. She does not trust me now. I feel it. The knowledge hurts a little. I take her home on Sunday night.

Outside the moon hangs, a yellow disc, above the cables and rooftops. Her hand is in mine, she smiles, and her eyes shine in the light from the 7/11. The Bearing train is full of Thai girls trying to escape their world. They can't touch us with their stares. I'm full of something so sweet, so bright, I'm burning through my clothes.

If she chose me to be her one and only I could be the man I always wanted to be. Her customers keep calling but tonight she belongs to me. Just tonight we are free.

I walk down the street to her gate. I stand in the light, a prisoner of the white lines on the road. She kisses me so sweetly goodnight.

I smoke a cigarette, alone but weightless and happy. This feeling cannot be bought. I have never seen her again.

Seven. Number 135 is haunted

She is six foot three in her heels and standing across Sukhumvit at the top of soi 5. You imagine her long body bent over an armchair, her big tits in your hands as you fuck her in the ass. A nano-second later she waves at someone, another farang, shit, shit, shit, you thought she was for sale. She is the most beautiful thing you have seen, and in Bangkok, that is more than just words. Diau, Diau, Diau. You will wait.

I see another farang watching her as she sees me and smiles as I step from the taxi and I breathe in, hooked. I had seen her Facebook pictures but I was not prepared for her eyes, mouth and stupendous tits. She is a totem pole of sex.

She stepped close to me and looked in my eyes. I stopped thinking which was unfortunate because she said, 'where we go?'

I just took her hand and walked down Sukhumvit in a stupor because all the blood had rushed from my head.

We sat in Gulliver's and I tried to determine if this ladyboy with a colossal body and stunning face was girlfriend material or not.

Nan seems bright and speaks good English so I ask her right there, 'What do you want?' Sure, I would never ask this question of a western girl on a first date but this is Bangkok where a first date, sex, love, betrayal and farewell can all happen in 24 hours, and probably will.

"I want boyfriend if I meet good man, can trust, not butterfly'. A well- rehearsed speech I suspect, but then I suspect everything, even my own motives.

A couple of relaxing drinks later and we share our potted, condensed, sanitized little biographies. It's always a depressing point in the proceedings that take place at the outset of any affair, liaison, love affair or encounter. The life story offered prior to going to a short time room may brief:

Ladyboy: Where you come from? Farang: England, Australia, USA, Switzerland (sorry if I missed you out)

Ladyboy: How long you stay Thailand?

Farang: 1 week, 2 weeks, too long

Ladyboy: Take shower.

Farang: Suck my cock.

But it's still an introduction and tedious but just something that has to be gotten out of the way before the main events.

Nan tells me about a previous boyfriend who obviously broke her heart, don't we all. I tell her my sad little story but I don't linger as I want keep it light and I want to concentrate on her lips. At one point well into the second hour of our date she grabs my hand, looks me in the eyes and says, 'Dawid, I know you have ladyboy girlfriend work as prostitute before but all ladyboy not same, same. 'I can earning money more one month than you can earn in two. If we boyfriend and girlfriend I never asking you for money if I working Cascade I never asking money for sex from boyfriend, never. I do this job not for too long just to making money my future.' She has a degree in Marketing and talks about doing an MA.

We go to Nana and play pool, kiss, hold hands and get wasted together.

She's a crap pool player but I am even worse. I don't care. She presses her little ass into my groin and kisses my neck. I leave her on soi 4 with her friends at 2am. She is going to Climax probably to pick up a late punter. I go home alone but happy. She's intelligent, positive, sexy, tall, and likes me?

Later I saw Oil's ghost walking on the roof of the apartment opposite mine again. I watched her carrying her red light. She stopped walking and looked at me. She's been dead for more than six months. She jumped from Life, Sukhumvit near On-Nut after her world imploded. Her world with a farang boyfriend and a degree of love began to melt away and she wound up accepting 2,000 baht to fuck someone's girlfriend. At some point her reason began to melt away and she convinced herself I was her boyfriend even though I never touched her with either passion or enmity. Then came the walk from the customer's apartment on the 9th floor to the 6th and her last action; her death leap. She still has the prettiest face of any ladyboy I have seen but she keeps the Spirit house outside my place busy. I need an exorcism.

The next day Nan moves in and doesn't leave. That's the speed love affairs move in LOS. She smiles a lot and looks at me with mock anger whenever I disagree with her. I like that look how a cat likes cream. I could get fat on that look. Sometimes I think too much. I think about 'My Dom' tattooed on her perfect belly, I think about buying her things just to see her smile. I think about a future but catch my mind drifting towards the outfield. I see myself running towards the bleachers, looking back over my shoulder into a rain-filled sky. I make the catch and stand alone in the rain. I feel no elation. I am alone on the muddy field. There is no future; this is Bangkok.

She got some late night phone calls; customers, ex-boyfriends, lost souls burning up the Bangkok ozone with lonely buzzwords; baby, tamali u?, wait you, miss you, soon, how much?

I knew this horse didn't have legs from the first night. Just a matter of watching it come unhinged and trying to predict when and how crazy it will get before that happens.

I don't wait long.

Tearful, choking voices, some real, some not are forming behind her eyes as she tries to make me wear a lie. It doesn't fit but it dawns on me as she gets up steam that this is it, she's going. I watch her in silence as she begins to believe her own bullshit. She's scaring herself with her story about the ghost in my room. It hates her, makes noises and shouts at her when she is alone. She has to go to a temple for three days to cleanse herself. Maybe it's true or maybe she's going on a jaunt with a customer who wants the 'girlfriend experience' in Kho Samui or Phuket. Maybe she is going back to 'My Dom'.

My insides turn to liquid cement and as I follow her outside as she leaves I take back my St. Joan pendant from around her neck.

Our eyes meet and for a moment I see the girl of my dreams looking at me again.

But the cement hardens and my heart is on a pole stuck in that cement. I feel like road-kill.

My room is silent. I thank the ghost and as I drink from the naked whisky bottle, I see the red light waving from across the rooftops.

Nan's gone. I never see her again.

Eight. Ladyboys the Documentary

It was hot, fucking hot and humid and dark and I am sweating as I listen to question after question as we stand on Silom road together. In the way that only television people can, Charlie and Dee press on regardless, earnestly, sympathetically, apologetically but pressing on is what they must do because they are deep in the shit now. They have made a mistake and now they are making another while trying to undo the first. They are too deadline orientated to care that while they may be able to extract information about Thai ladyboys from inside of my head they will never be able to truly 'know' that knowledge; not in their bodies the way that I know. Knowing in the body is where it's at. Anything less than experiencing with the body is just 'talking the talk'. Now they are asking me to tell them precisely what 'walking the walk' means, assuming that I am able to do that.

That assumption is mistake number three, a repeat of mistake number one: asking questions without understanding the source of the answers and believing blindly what they are told.

After reading Bangkok Baby, they have asked me to be the technical adviser for a documentary about Thai ladyboys and tonight they are lucky. I know some of the answers and all of the questions. The where, what, why, and how of ladyboys is galloped through without pause, without understanding. It's becoming tedious. Then just like that, the night snapped its fingers and the quality of the darkness changed and the creatures of the night begin to appear. So intent are they on asking me about ladyboys that a tall, dark, red-lipped urchin walks past and they do not see her, only her wake. 'How can you tell?', they ask me. 'How can you not?', I ask back at them, 'Are you both blind'? A ladyboy who looks like she has been working late in an office crosses Silom, walking behind them and as she mounts the steps to the BTS. She hovers in my eye-line for a moment longer than necessary. We smile, recognize, imagine, taste. For some reason that I still don't really understand the TV people are open-mouthed. 'That's how it's done', I tell them. 'Its just human attraction and it happens all over the world, it just happens quicker here in Bangkok.

Sometimes it happens too quickly'. I know they don't understand what I mean. But they begin to sense the mojo of Bangkok and how the city will carry your heart if you let yourself be carried away. Now they begin to see it, the city opens itself to them as more and more ladyboys walk past us almost on cue as if this was all a surreal opera about vampires. I begin to dream, to enter the waking dream world where the senses are everything and sense nothing. No questions are needed because now they can feel the night but still they ask, 'Why do ladyboys like you so much, how do they know you like them', a portent of the many embarrassing questions that were soon to come my way. We all like to feel we are special but that's just a kind of fantasy not something tangible we can talk about. It's not real. 'I don't think I am special. Ladyboys are just horny little devils who want to stick their horns in me'.

'I'm not special, I'm just available', I laugh, overcompensating. 'Probably all ladyboys want a boyfriend. Once they know I live here it's easy. If you live here everything changes; the way Thai people talk to you changes. Even those who are prostitutes dream about a lover, a friend, a partner, someone who cares about them. Ladyboys may be uber-women but they are human like the rest of us, they get lonely, horny, miss their families, dream. Are you sure, they seem to be thinking.

'Basically, we are in the shit.'

'Because of what you told us about Tom we don't want to use him in the film but as the director, Cathy says, nobody who knows about ladyboys will talk to us, without him we have nothing. We are fucked David. We are getting death threats from some people because of Tom. We are like lepers now. We don't want Tom but what can we do? Tom was a guy that the TV company people had pencilled in to be the star of a new series about Thai ladyboys. He was revealed to be barking mad despite the psychological testing done by the TV people.

I say nothing. 'Can you help?' Like a Patpong whore when the customer asks, 'How much', I begin to weigh the possible outcomes. 'Up to you', I tell them with a straight face. It works just as well for me as it does for the whores.

I wait some more 'Ok, if we dumped Tom would you help us?' 'Maybe

I could speak to a friend of mine', I say.

In the morning Charlie the producer calls. 'Tom is history'.

We want you to be in the documentary. Will you do it? 'Ok, ok', I say wishing I hadn't.

I call Annie.

It's a day for making decisions. I want her back in my life.

All along the Chao Phrya bridges are beginning to burn.

Nine. A Year

When the sun died and the hot winds blew me to desolation last August there was little hope and nothing to anticipate. The smouldering autumn sank through Sukhumvit and my heart was hollow and dry and as empty as the soi 4 bars. When the tourists leave Bangkok changes her colours to grey. Free of Farida, free of all but the sharpest of pain and regret I haunt the bars of Sukhumvit and think of an England that's easy to idealise.

The Ladyboys arrived at Nana just as always but some had a harried look on their sweet faces.

The traffic was less of a factor when crossing the road and the girls in the bars at the Nana mouth stared with dreamy, unfocused eyes at the giant advertising hoarding above the soi. CPS was having a sale; 70% off.

I remember her narrow hips and wide shoulders swing before me as we walk toward soi 2 to catch a taxi home.

Home. Where is that?

Perhaps it is in her body, her mannish sexuality and her feminine softness, her breasts; too perfect to be real, her svelte, panther-like, rock and roll saunter.

Although once I was certain it was true, today I know it was never so. The rain comes every day and after it the sun. I am tired of the autumn humidity. The hot, acrid smoke from burning oil mingles with the steam from a noodle shop making me feel like I am walking through choking soup instead of air.

That night, the August sky had a heavy, dangerous look and the lights of the staggering condominiums that leant over soi 6 seemed to offer small hope.

Like cheap Christmas lanterns they cannot reach into the dark pit of the gathering night. What would this night bring to my small acre of Bangkok?

I remember Surin city when she gave her offerings to the monks on the celebration of her twenty-fifth birthday, her third cycle. I was so lost I almost asked them for some guidance.

In truth, I couldn't even hand them the parcels she and her mother had made when they asked if I wanted to do so. I would have felt such a fake. The whole affair reminded me of feeding elephants at the zoo.

I was dispossessed of her. Already gone. The contradiction between tough, ladyboy and supplicant is mysterious. If ladyboys got organised they could rule the country; sexy and softly persuasive but with a male sex drive. I blame the hormones on their demise. It ends all ambition. So instead of scaling the social ladder they live alone in a variety of haunts and manners. Neung was thrown out of her apartment for playing loud music, Beer found a boyfriend and her life changed for a week or two and Farida tries to grow flowers on her windowsill. 'Beauty keep my heart good', she says.

Their little rooms are often bright and colourful places and you may be surprised to know that many keep fish for the same reason they like flowers and pretty, childish bedcovers and teddy bears.

It's a lonely world on the outside.

Now the last grey rains of October fold their sullen wings and a tuneless music begins to drift across Khlong San's night gardens.

A broken music of hopeless things tried and failed. What am I doing here?

He sits alone sipping green Fanta. When asked if he is well, he answers that despite his years and years of living in the kingdom, doing so, he could only be well. The uniquely ticklish colour and oddity of green Fanta makes me smile, makes my heart shudder again into life like an old car starting after a long abandonment. I thank the white-haired gent born of the only 60's war to count, and leave, a little lighter. Something small, a green crocus is growing. Is it hope?

The brilliant spars that span Chong Nonsi reflect light from the myriad windows in the now empty rooms of skyscrapers.

A spider; dreamed by artists and sanctioned by dishonest politicians. How does Art and commerce exist here in such a freewheeling, corrupt and random swamp? Welcome to Thailand.

Just a station or two from the Airport expressway but overlooked by all. The farang landmark map is blind to its beauty. Sukhumvit and Silom exert to strong a power. They say, 'come and see all that is forbidden'. Khao San road tells its lies year after year. 'Come and see the 'authentic' Bangkok. It will sing its siren song as long as there are over-privileged 'gappers'. They make you want to spew. Colonial parasites.

Laughing at the hookers, pretending they would never pay for it. But behind closed doors, a different story is written. It is written in lipstick on their hotel room mirrors. Everybody pays. We all pay, one way or another.

Farida calls me for no reason but that she knows now it is over. Sadness in her voice betrays her loss, but she has waited too long. I am free. I am empty of her now and the night sky encloses my fall from that position of grace to which love lifts us into an uncertain future.

As I plunge through the frigid but refreshing wind a divine hand twists the kaleidoscope that carries our lives and I can see that beside the holy wars and worldwide suffering that ours is just a little sorrow. Yet the pain is none less sharp, the memories no less powerful. She asks after me in constrained, awkward tones and I, numb with sensations I cannot express, futile with tenderness but anger too want to tell her, if only she could understand, that I won't forget. I want to tell her, with mixed emotions of bitterness and love, that when I think of her holy music plays aloud that she can never hear.

Though she may forget me, she filled my life with emotions so sharp and vivid that although I now reject that gift she gave, I won't forget.

Ten. Annie

That green shoot of last September has grown and Annie is become my joy, full of childish happiness beyond reason or measure and of darker passions that sustain. It's her birthday next month and so I thank God for Green Fanta and it's illogical purity, it's tiny, everyday miracle that grows and grows. But it almost never happened.

She called as you were leaving work one night back in August 'I littel bit drunk Dawid, I dlink whiskey wid my flend, is ok, you not angry?' Not angry you arrive to collect her. She totters down the steps on killer heels and displaying killer tits as only ladyboys can. She falls asleep with her head in your lap before you get home and then fucks and sleeps, fucks and sleeps. You remember thinking, 'This ain't rock n roll, this is something else, something more insidious'.

Pattaya, September. You have gone to fetch her back to Bangkok realising you want to be with her but the face and eyes looking at you from behind tinted glasses are haunted and distant. The opposite of the Annie you know. She reaches for the lighter that waits on the table between you and burns the cellophane from the top of the Marlboro packet. You find this disturbing.

That night you fetch her clothes from her friend who watches, smoking just out of your line of sight. It's her room where Annie has been holed up in sin city. When you stopped calling her, she left town and the floods behind. She left her disappointment in you behind and found her old friend Ice/Yabba, the crazy medicine had been waiting for her all along.

In his hotel room Travis and you have it covered. He reads from the battered book of bitter experience and tells you what you face in rescuing her. Annie's friend Poo waits with Travis while you collect Annie's things and uses him like the slut he is. Together, you and Annie climb to several squalid landings in a squalid building where you meet several squalid ladyboys as if the building were a part of the YWCA or should it be YMCA in hell?

Annie knows them all as they walk up or downstairs in slippers, pyjamas or less. They all have distant stares, absent and empty. Ice is in the house. Ice is the house. Ice house, Pattaya Beach, Paradise, Thailand.

She wants one hit from the pipe before you leave. You say, 'Go ahead, see you!' She begs you not to go but the sweltering doorknob leaps into your hand and you are looking down a slippery slope broken by concrete steps. She believes you now and comes down behind on the devil's high heels, 'clack, shout, clack, shout', until you are both outside and facing one another.

You imagine frost and twin plumes of misty breath but there are none. There is only the tropical heat and the insects that rasp madly in the trees; a vocal audience to your indecision.

'Why you leave me alone only because I smoke little bit, I love you sooo much Dawid and want stay wid you too much, why you want leave me again?'

The insects seem to get louder, drowning your thoughts, smothering you. Something bad is happening and they are shouting something you can't make out. You feel yourself zoning out and then Annie grabs you by the shirt and slaps you across the face so hard your ears ring. When she was fourteen years old her father took her from Petchabun to Koh Samui, and left her there. Frustrated in his attempts to interest her in Muay- Thai, or any other manly pastimes he asked her what she wanted to do. She said, 'dance', and when she tells you she does a little twirl and throws her hands up and says, 'La, La, La' in a way that only Ladyboys can do. So her father got her a job in a Ladyboy revue bar owned by a Dutchman and his Ladyboy girlfriend.

'So were you fucking farangs at fourteen', I ask. 'No' . . .she says, incredulous that I would think such a thing, 'cannot doo'!!

'Cannot get ID card until fifteen yr old, Dawid'!

She tells you later, when you stop laughing for reasons she does not understand, that in fact, her job description included dancing in a nightly cabaret like Salazar or Tiffany's. Not so bad, except that she was only fourteen. 'I not go with customer, I not know about sex then. One time man ask for my number from bar and boss say I can meet if I want if I not come late for work. I not speak English, can only say hello, thank you and my name Ann. I am 15 year old there. He take me shopping and eat dinner together. The next day he give me some money and he come every night see my show and when he see me sing or dance he tip everybody very good. When him go home he send me 40,000 baht for two month after he go. He tell me he love me but not have sex him.'

She stayed in Samui for four years then she went to Pattaya. She stayed only one month. Then Exe, her best friend in Pattaya bought her to Guess Bar in Bangkok. A Swiss boyfriend later and a few months of guessing customers weight on soi 4, then she quit the scene and later she met me. She told me that she did not want to 'sell her body more'. Quitting is not simple. No-one wants a girl to quit the bar scene.

159

Her friends want her back, the more people do their job, the more 'normal' it is. Customers don't want a girl to quit. Facebook heroes are endlessly asking for a webcam date or a message to brighten their non-Thai existences. A slip back into that world is just an argument away; for both of us. Annie's evolution from boy to androgynous dancer, prostitute and TV personality has been surprising, challenging, heartbreaking and exciting in equal measure. Annie's use of drugs along the way is no surprise and probably 70-80% of ladyboys and girls that are involved in prostitution even to a small degree are touched by it's soul- crushing influence. She is a fighter and so are most ladyboys. That's one of the reasons for my admiration of trangender people everywhere.

Eleven. Cha-am New Year

Annie's tight, round ass is rolling in time with the Isaan music blasting across the seated throng. You hold her hips clad in her little denim shorts. She dances raising her hands in the archetypal V sign adopted by all Thai people. She thrusts her ass in your face, laughs and tells you she loves you as you kiss and drink together. You cannot compete with her in the eyes of the watching crowd. Your farang statehood usually draws all eyes but tonight this ladyboy is stealing the show.

Tonight you are the Base and she is the Flyer. She is the entertainment and you are the support she needs. Like all exciting dancers she needs to feel something solid beneath her, holding her, loving her. You like this job.

You realise that you love her and that the horror and pain of the last few months is almost forgotten.

Perhaps not forgotten but accepted, resolved in part and without the sharp pangs of heartache and sadness that have been flooding your emotional landscape for as long as you can remember. Tonight you feel you are waking from a bad dream and like the rest of Thailand, drying out after the floods. The morning light no longer seems so depressing. She smiles, 'I love you so much my husband, I love YOU'! She shouts over the music. You smile. You believe her. That's a new experience. In Cha-am we stay on soi 2 in Tonys Guest House. Tony is a Danish guy and is married to a Thai woman. They have two daughters. He met her online and they married a year later.

They seem happy together. They have pictures of Jesus and Buddha everywhere and they are shocked when I thank them for their warmth and hospitality. They don't understand why some people may not be so generous towards a man and his ladyboy girlfriend. It's touchingly naïve. The room is huge, clean and airy and 500 baht a night even during the New Year holiday. We rent a motorcycle from Tony for 100 baht a day and tour the town, the beach and the temple.

We ride our rented motorcycle to the isolated temple in Cha-am and take sexy photos next to the Ganesh statue, blasphemers that we are. Ordinary happiness like this is hard to find 'ordinary' is dangerous because it can fall apart so easily especially if you begin to believe your own promises. Believe the promises of a ladyboy if you want, but never, listen to your own. I never enjoyed magic shows as a kid. I always wanted to unveil the illusion but Bangkok has taught me to go along with the ride for as long as it lasts. So now I will admit to being a fan of hers and I will resist pulling the beautiful wings off this strange creature we have found and I confess that I need a 'good' mistake. I am neither a bad man nor a good man but I am on a road that no-one ever knows well, so Annie, promise me one thing. No promises, okay? Just don't make any promises because I know you can't keep them. See, I've listened before to promises and that's why I am here talking to the bedroom wall and waiting for you to come from the shower and fill up my heart with all those promises that I love so much.

Twelve. Moscow on the Beach

The lights of Pattaya reflect off the water and add colour to the velvet blackness of the night. It's one am and the rooftop pool is a languid green. It's a tiny lagoon about 12 metres square amid surrounding hotels thrusting toward the sky. I am thrusting into the sweetest little ladyboy I have ever had.

The Pattaya city lights seem to match our action, changing colour and glowing as we are glowing in the darkness. We are sending out sparks. Getting caught snogging in the lift by a fat Muscovite and his fatter wife gives me no end of amusement and for the first time in Pattaya we make a Russian look away. England 2, Russia 0.

Back on 2nd road another Russian steps so close to me that I say, 'what do you want?' He looks surprised. There are so many of them and they are everywhere. This is no longer 'our' place. The Western star is waning. The Slavs all stare and stare with no sense of grace or warmth or even sentience. They stare at Annie because they have never seen anything like her and they stare at me because in their own hideous country anyone different is likely to be hunted down and attacked. Physically handicapped people, gays and people of colour stay indoors. Neo-Nazi skinhead groups roam the streets of Moscow looking for someone to vent their anger, frustration and dissolution on. I asked a Russian girl whom I had the experience of some time ago why there were no handicapped people on the streets of Moscow. 'Why would they want to show themselves', she said!

Fooling around in the pool I told Annie she had no respect and teasing me back she floated onto her back and lifting both feet out of the water placed them together as if they were her hands. 'Sawasdee Ka', she said, laughing and making me laugh too. The truth is though that even the rudest of Thais have so much more respect and good grace than the Slavs. Annie does not like Russians either.

She was even able to tell the difference when two guys were staring at her through the McCafe window. Despite their stares, when we got up to leave they smiled and waved goodbye. Annie said,' They Farang, not Russian, they have malayad'! (respect)

Walking through the throngs of sunburnt Russians on Beach road is to be recommended if you are drunk on Siam Sato and easily angered. Sato tastes like strong, white wine but costs 25 baht for a large bottle the same size as a big bottle of Leo. It's a hangover in a bottle but just too good. The tourists stare with a mixture of disgust and fear. I stare back, on the street, in the 7/11 as they openly nudge each other and gossip. This is not Bangkok and I know I am not going to put up with this for long. We get off the street and sit down to eat in a typical Thai place. Outside at a polished steel table are a young couple. Hippy dress, piercings, braided hair. They look like they belong on Khao San road not here with the package tourists. They stare at us the whole time we are ordering our food. When I go out for cigarette, he approaches me for a light. Tentatively he says, 'Excuse me, you know your girlfriend is not real girl' in a thick Russian accent. I tell him 'Yes'. He says he just wanted to be sure I knew. He thought he was being a Good Samaritan. 'She's my girlfriend, we live together in Bangkok. I know she is not a girl, she's better than a girl,' I tell him.

He smiles, 'Ok', no problem. He was young enough to imagine that while he and his equally young girlfriend could recognise a ladyboy, I, in my dotage, obviously, could not. They were nice people, we chatted for a little while. They left. I learned a lesson. Only 98% of Russians are as ignorant as dogs.

Back in Bangkok and it is Chinese New Year.

The afternoon comes around quickly and we spend it eating, laughing and generally doing little. Annie has a whole bank of phrases and words that I love to hear her say. When she thinks someone might disapprove of her she tosses her hair, makes a face and says, 'Sobut Bob', at least that's what it sounds like. It means something like, 'up to them, I not care'. I love it when she does this.

We take a trip to Chinatown. She strolls by my side, getting deeper under my skin with every step she takes.

Flayed animals of every variety are hanging outside food shops on Yanowat road, and she refuses to look. 'Kidiak', she says, 'it makes me sick'. We laugh and 'saluwan', tease and play jokes on each other and laugh so much beer comes out of my nose.

Our latest fun insults for each other are 'Song On'. This means 'soft pack'. You can say it when you ask for cigarette's but it's also a bit like saying, 'soft lad' or another is 'Num-num On'; 'soft young man! Probably not strictly Thai! 'Sop Maa', is another useful insult for your Thai ladyboy girlfriend if she looks a bit rough one day. It means 'dead dog'.

E heah or E sat are other good ones; 'bitch' or 'E sat kon chan', 'my bitch'. She constantly asks me 'Why you i-hear'? 'Why are you a bastard?' 'E' is the feminine pronoun of 'You' and 'I' the male. Often it feels as if we are two people not separated by a culture that rejects her as 'inauspicious' and me as 'farang'. In Thailand the number nine is very 'auspicious'. Our apartment is 27, added together they make nine. But this 'girl' walking by my side, waiting for me when I come home; she's my lucky number, my fortune cookie. She's my good mistake, My Slumdog Princess.

Thirteen. Searching for 'Sabai'

I look at her one last time before leaving. Her smooth skin, provocative neo- amazonian jaw-line and her bottom, stealing from beneath the covers like my favourite little moon. A glimpse of pubic hair on a round little olive belly as the music begins playing through my earphones and I close the door on the best girl I have ever known.

Pearl Jam suck me back in time and give me cause to compare my first effort at love in Bangkok to today's ease of heart. Their words hold no pain now, their blowtorch flame burnt out by a brighter but gentler light. Sheets of empty canvas. Untouched sheets of clay. Lay spread out before me as her body once did.

In the West, the girl wrapped in my sheets would be referred to as enigmatic because she could not be understood. But she is complicated only as Rubik's famous cube is complicated. Her complications and contradictions do not come from within and while she may be a puzzle to others she is not to herself.

All five horizons revolved around her soul As the earth to the sun. Now the air I taste and I breathe Has taken a turn.

A woman is exercising alone in the entrance to a food court. Her moves are part Thai-Chi, part step aerobic. She is someone's grandmother.

A monk is begging for alms from a tiger skin clad woman in dark glasses sitting at a bus stop. She is politely refusing his appeals. Thailand is never what it seems.

The guide-book Thailand is just a 'rule of thumb', a kindergarten sum of its parts. There is only one rule of living here; sabai. It means a combination of happiness and ease of heart. It's a harder lesson to learn, because of its apparent simplicity. It is a lesson that must be learned in the body not with a questioning, questing intellect. Sophistry cannot solve this riddle. One must cross the Rubicon and 'see' only in looking back.

The picture of the king is twenty-five metres high, a kind of towering moral teacher, he reminds me of a Stalin of a different doctrine.

Around the corner I am confronted by my bête-noir.

He is approaching me with a ready smile and already unhooking his battered white helmet from the handlebar of his motorcycle.

He is a dumpy looking Thai, short in the leg and stout but his fingernails reflect the sunlight in pink shades. One evening, Annie and I, coming home from some debauchery on Sukhumvit beckoned to the moto-riding ex cons waiting in the shadows of the Exon building along Phaholyothin road.

Annie immediately mounted behind by our man and after some rapid checking of the tyre pressure and ground clearance designed to bump up the price later, I climbed aboard another motosyc.

Annie got to our den in the woods before me and was laughing as the taxis drove away together.

'He ladyboy', she said. 'He tell me I very lucky have good boyfriend, he say he have but not good Thai man, treat him bad.' She has said this in a rush, without pause in her excitement and I can't understand who is the ladyboy she is speaking about. 'He, the taxi driver'. 'He is not a ladyboy', I say, I saw him, he is just a gay man'. She takes a mockingly deep breath and sighs at me. Ladyboys themselves consider males in any state of transition toward female a ladyboy, even those we would consider camp, gay men in the west. Every day as I travel to work the same 'ladyboy' moto rider is waiting for me. I am not made happy by this daily occurrence. His motorbike is the oldest of the fleet; bent foot-pegs and a battered, tiny seat. It feels like sitting on a knife blade, albeit, wrapped in a tissue.

As he approached me today I found myself enviously eying the other motorbikes and thinking, 'Why can't I go to work on that one?'

Then it hits me that what I am experiencing is 'Greng- Jai'.It is that much discussed and argued about cultural peculiarity that forces me to shudder through the bones of my ass on every bump we ride over. I don't want to offend the guy by asking for another taxi.

I realise that this feels a little like 'English politeness' and another small wormhole of cultural assimilation has been mined in my farang brain and more crucially, felt in my body!

I travel by motorcycle far more frequently now as this is less frustrating than taxis, that are, at least in my experience, safer, but stress inducing. Annie and I made a flying visit to Pattaya a few months ago and took little luggage with us. We caught two motorsycs at the bus station and spent 15 minutes racing each other to the Soi Bukaow area. Dangerously diving in and out of traffic and overtaking each other, the riders got competitive. It was crazy fun but just don't pick a motorcycle driver with the number four.

Its inauspicious as it's supposed to be the number of death. Although in that context it may be a lucky thing? After all, the driver is not dead is he! Bangkok meter taxi drivers are frustrating because they are often just crooked enough to fool you while not making you actually get out of the vehicle. Once I learned my way to a few locations I began to notice some taxis choosing to take the least useful route to get somewhere. An example happened one night when Annie and I wanted to go to Sukhumvit 22 from Krunthonburi. The route that is simple and quick is along Rama 2 and up 22 from the south end, not along Sukhumvit. I told the driver to go this way but he ignored me and when I said in very bad Thai, 'tamai aom, bi Sukhumvit?' 'Why are you going around and going along Sukhumvit Road', he said the traffic bad the way I tell him. Annie did not speak and I wondered why Thai girls and ladyboys seem to have deference to taxi drivers while in the West we would not put up with it. Sitting in the traffic that the driver said he was avoiding I had had enough. I had asked Annie to tell him to go the other way but she remained silent.

In the traffic jam, I took Annie's hand and got out of the taxi. I gave him 100 baht as the meter showed 95 baht. The usual cost of this trip is 68baht!!

When we got on the street I asked Annie why she had not told the driver to go the way we wanted. She was white with suppressed anger. 'Cannot, I not want problem because angry too much' She had been angry the whole time but kept silent. I told her that if she had told me as much I would have stopped the taxi as soon as I saw him go the wrong way. She said, 'Ok, next time I say to you'.

She knew that having asked the driver to go the way we wanted once, any further instruction or complaint would have sparked angry words or more. She did not try, choosing to employ 'Sam Ruam' or control of the emotions. Perhaps to Thais there is no middle ground as far as the emotions go. Unlike foreigners who can shout, laugh, cry and fight one hour only to be in the opposite state the next, Thais do not want to risk losing control because those emotions belong to the individual. They are not for others to see and if they do the consequences can be extreme.

Fourteen. The Promise

The filming of Lady boys is just beginning and when I asked Annie how she would tell our story she said, 'If ask me, I tell about when we meet Facebook and give number and then we meet and eating together. It romantic. I think you handsum but butterfly man. No, maybe helicopter man.'

'Annie, I don't think you understand . . . I mean do you remember the first time we talked to the TV crew about their idea to make the documentary about Ladyboys?' Annie says, 'I think like Thai movie, I make before.'

Me: Oh yeah, let me guess . . .

Annie: No, boxing your mouth. Never do like dat. They give we card have words we only say same as this but NO, not same. I make movie before at school about students at school. I was scared little bit first we meet because I think I cannot talk English very good about how I can make them know what are my feelings. I remember we argue but I know when we go out we are working and not same in room.

Me: Ha, Ha. Yes, I know you got angry about the photo you saw on the camera when we were at the temple on the first day of filming. They asked me why you walked away and didn't eat with us. I told them you saw a picture of Nan's underwear and her number '135' badge from Cascades.

Annie: They ask me about this same you. I tell them I not angry you. Jealous little bit but not angry. I cannot be angry you teerak. Me: This day, I know I love you more, because you have a good heart about this picture. The director asked me if you go home, and if we have to finish filming because you are angry and jealous. She asked me to go and find you and make everything ok.

I told her I would leave you stay alone for little time and you be ok because you are a good person.

Annie: 'I not go home because look like stupid person I do dat! I only jealous.'

My memory of events begins with a feeling of responsibility. The strange thing about television is that although one may never actually believe it to be true, because of the power of the media one is elected spokesperson for an entire culture, faction, nationality or group. It can be overpowering.

You come alive with the red light on the camera. This is familiar. This is easy. Dangerous static is buzzing in your head but your mouth is not listening. Your mouth cannot stop because so much is expected of it. Words are expected to issue from your mouth.

Wise, foolish, arrogant, damaging, life changing words. The camera does not care. The buzz is dampened only momentarily by your internal bravery speech. 'I am doing this for the greater good'. The camera is a drug. You talk, talk, talk and the camera sucks you into its hungry mouth. The static buzz grows in volume and forms itself into the collective voices of those wiser than you, the voices of the betrayed, the damaged, those who have a life at stake and those who simply know more.

Two years in Thailand and you are sounding like the oracle of all wisdom.

As the words leaving your mouth compose themselves into sentences and allow space for the pauses and the gesticulations that support them in their attempt at truth and knowledge. You know the picture they are painting is a fake. How could it be anything else? You are not a kathoey. You are not Thai. You loved a girl for some months and it went bad. How little you know.

Standing behind the camera and visible only in the spotlights glare you see an army of the dead and living. They are watching. Distracted, you raise a hand to shield your eyes and see better the faces of your accusers. Oil, the ladyboy who jumped from the 6th floor of Sukhumvit Life is there. Are you telling her story in which she was dumped by a farang lover again and again and in which the starring role goes to ice/yabba? Her crazed phone calls and her delusion that you were her boyfriend; are you talking about that. Are you talking about the ghosts like her that jumped?

Whose story is this? Is it hers? The one to whom your thoughts turn when a certain mood overtakes you, the ghost that you cannot look at, because you're not brave enough?

There you go again, another sweeping generalization and a generous sweep of the arm to embed that small truth in the mind of the viewing public. You are an asshole, an asshole with a big mouth. The faces of the ghosts and the living are tight lipped in agreement. They mouth the word, 'asshole' as you talk and talk.

You have been chosen by fate and opportunism to speak in their place and you're fucking it up for them. For the Irish, Swiss, Slovenian, English and American lovers of ladyboys long dead or living all with the same sad story.

But stories are always sad at the end. Just like life, they end with a disappearance, a fading out or an abrupt stop like hitting the concrete at the end of a long fall; messy and sad. You know about messy, sad relationships that stop abruptly. You are the master of messy endings.

The ghosts fall silent as a bright light appears amongst them. It's an angel. The light grows brighter as she walks into the smaller light cast on you by the camera and the fruit vendors stall. You are not alone as you squirm on the hook.

Annie is standing by your side with all the happy energy a twenty one year old ladyboy can share. She holds your hand and whispers, 'teerak'. You say, 'Hi baby' as the camera records your first meeting for the third time that night at Thonglor. The farang living and the ghosts mime your words, 'Hi baby', as the ladyboy dead whisper, 'teerak', alive again with hope, love and possibility.

Even Siraporn comes from her lonely room and from sticking sequins on the her Barbie prom queen, 'teerak', she says and you realize that the living and the dead do not see you and Annie but instead see their lost ones, the dead or the forgotten. They see again those against whose caresses they have hardened their hearts. They see them as they saw them the first time they met and fell in love at the BTS at the bar or on the streets of the city before a messy ending had even been considered. Alive again, you hold Annie's hand, swallow and speak now with the strength of a thousand voices, about love and ladyboys about beginnings and possibilities.

Made in the USA
Middletown, DE
16 December 2022

18816777R00102